Long Long Ago

a love story that is true

1967

LISELOTTE METTLER &
ELWIN WALLACE LAW

This Book is dedicated
By both of us
To the gift of Love

"Long, Long Ago"

Long, long ago
I saw you sitting there

With your beautiful face and smile
And lovely golden hair

I asked permission to sit down
And wondered what you'd say
Across your face came a slight frown
But your smile said please stay

WINTER OF 1967: ARRIVAL IN GERMANY

▶ This is a true story that begins in Frankfurt, Germany, in the year 1967. Lyndon B. Johnson was President, the Vietnam War was raging, and I was twenty-nine.

It was a gray and rainy evening as the train pulled into the station of Frankfurt, about 5:00, and came to a screeching halt. I could see the pillows of steam from the engine and the bustling people with their bags crowding each other, faces intent on reaching their individual destinations. There were few smiles or pleasantries exchanged. Everyone seemed to be on his or her own mission to somewhere. Off in the distance a young man and woman embraced as they said good-bye. It was all strangely exciting.

I had just received a wonderful position as regional manager of the Ruhr Gebiet around Düsseldorf and Köln with an investment company out of Los Angeles, California. I was taking the train to Munich to our headquarters, and this was only a short stop in Frankfurt for an hour or so. I found a restaurant in the train station where I could enjoy a wonderful German beer and relax. As I entered the front door, one could hear German music in the background (thankfully not too loud). I looked around and was surprised—the restaurant was practically empty except for a table by the wall where a beautiful, blonde German girl was sitting, reading a book. I thought I had nothing to lose and approached her and asked in English, or maybe in broken German, if I might sit down.

I detected a curious look cross her face, but she smiled and said yes.

"My name is John," I said. I explained that John was a nickname, and that my real name was Elwin. "Mine is Liselotte," she replied with a beautiful accent, "but I am called Lisa." We immediately started a conversation. She spoke perfect English as well as four other languages, and I had fun practicing my partial German, which I could communicate to some degree. I was dressed in a gray business suit with a tie, and she had on a smart looking casual blue skirt with a white sweater. She was quite beautiful and most engaging. There was an ease and flow to our conversation. We spoke for nearly an hour, not really knowing where the time went. I learned that she had just completed medical school and had received her degree in Kiel, in northern Germany, where she was doing her residency. Somewhere along the way she gave me her phone number and address in Stuttgart where she was visiting her mother. She glanced at her watch and said her train was about to leave. I later came to find out she tends to wait until the very last minute in nearly everything, but somehow always manages beautifully. I walked rapidly with her to the train, and we politely and properly said our good-byes.

On the train to Munich, I could not get her out of my mind. The ease, the fun, the interest, and the excitement all seemed to blend together. A week went by and I knew I had to try to find her. I bought a ticket to Stuttgart and appeared unannounced at her front door. I rang the bell, and I could hear her call to her mother that she would answer the door. When she saw me she seemed quite startled, but pleased. She gave me that beautiful smile and asked what I was doing there. I explained that I had hoped we could continue the conversation we had in Frankfurt. She could not help but laugh. I told her the only reason I had not called was that I was afraid she might say, "No, do not come." She knew I wanted to see her again.

After introducing me to her mother, who was a delightful lady, we sat in the living room and had some tea and wonderful German cake, which Lisa had made. Lisa and I kept exchanging glances, and finally I asked if she could show me a bit of Stuttgart. She agreed and I said a polite auf Wiedersehen to her mother, who seemed to get a kick out of my broken German. We drove into the city with Lisa's yellow Volkswagen bug; little did I know how important this car would become over the coming months. Lisa pointed out many historical points of interest. We parked the car, walked to a museum, and found ourselves standing in a crowded line. Lisa had a lovely form-fitting red dress, and I found myself, from time to time, slightly pressing against her. I suppose I was conspicuous. Somehow there seemed to be a strange, yet familiar knowing, almost a recognition between us. We both found ourselves quite attracted to one another standing there in that crowded line of culture.

When we finally returned to her home, I could not resist holding her and kissing that beautiful mouth. After a few words and unspoken recognition of what we were feeling, we went into her room, closed the door, and made beautiful and intimate love. The fact that we had just met for a second time did not seem to matter. It was as if we had known each other somewhere before. From time to time, I thought of her mother, but was assured we would be left alone, or at least she thought so. It never can be certain at a time like that.

Over the ensuing weeks and months, we fell very much in love. Lisa was the most positive and optimistic person I had ever known. She had something genuinely innate. Nearly every weekend she would come to my apartment in Munich, and as I travelled throughout Germany on business during the week, I would meet her whenever I could.

We had great fun together skiing on the slopes of Garmisch, walking in the English Gardens in Munich, attending the rowdy Oktoberfest and enjoying beer and wine together, as well as sailing at Chiemsee, south of Munich. It was a fun, adventurous, and loving relationship. Everything seemed perfect: I had established a wonderful position in the top-producing area in Europe's investment world, and she had her medical career in front of her, which she loved.

LISA MEETS JOHN FOR THE FIRST TIME

▶▶ I had just started my residency training at the Department of Obstetrics and Gynecology at Kiel University in Germany, and had just returned from a sixteen-month period in the Peruvian jungle. I had selected gynecology because the chairman of the department in Kiel had accepted me without seeing my papers, as he seemed to be fascinated by someone who had worked in the jungle. My other choices were pediatrics and ophthalmology. I had worked in the Amazon Hospital Albert Schweitzer in the *selva baja* (the flat jungle), and felt the urgent need to get specialized in a medical field in order to possibly return to my jungle hospital with more specific knowledge in order to really help people. The strict rules of the Kiel University Hospital frightened me; politically, I was very much on the communistic-socialistic side and wanted equality and equal opportunities for everyone.

It was the time of the uprising of a huge group of young German students and particularly intellectuals against the establishment. I had participated in a march of doctors against new rules to restrict our working hours; we did not want higher salaries nor did we want to work less; our wishes were very much to the contrary. After only two weeks in Kiel, I went home by train to see my mother and brother and had to change trains in Frankfurt for Stuttgart. In a restaurant at the train station I had ordered tea and was reading about Che Guevara, whom I had met in Argentina in 1962 and who was one of my heroes. He had just been killed on October 9, 1967, in Bolivia. Although later I understood many of my political misconceptions, in 1967 I was very much on the left side and was shocked by his death.

As this tall, good-looking American (I spotted his origin immediately), addressed me and asked if he could sit down, I wanted to say no, but when I saw that the whole restaurant was empty, I could only smile and say yes. He was polite, handsome, and well-dressed, and perhaps he needed some directions. We talked about many things, and I certainly found him to be on the sunny side of life—totally unaware of the political turmoil we were experiencing in 1967. He did not yet have a home in Germany, but was eager to learn how things were, as he had been away for some years. Previously, he had spent two years with the American Army in 1962 to '63, in Germany. He had, however, no extensive knowledge of the revolution or leaders like Che Guevara. Well, I just recall what I was reading in a dispatch to *The Guardian* written by the journalist Richard Gott on the day of Che Guevara's death: "It was difficult to recall that this man had once been one of the great figures of Latin America. It was not just that he was a great guerrilla leader; he had been a friend of presidents as well as revolutionaries. His voice had been heard and appreciated in inter-American councils as well as in the jungle. He was a doctor, an amateur economist, once Minister of Industries in revolutionary Cuba, and Castro's right-hand man. He may well go down in history as the greatest continental figure since Bolivar. Legends will be created around his name."

Let me recall here some of my memories of Che, who I met in the outskirts of Tucuman in Argentina in 1963. At that time, he was already in power in Cuba, but still had the sensibility of a medical doctor and met with groups in his native Argentina. I was then with an international student exchange program in Argentina and spent a few days with Che. I learned that in 1950 he travelled alone in northern Argentina and wrote a diary of this bicycle trip on the hoof. This diary revealed his early concern for those who lived below the poverty line. Because he was a medical student traveling with hardly any money, he asked for lodgings at hospitals and police stations, from which he observed this other Argentina.

The unrevised diaries of his first trip across Latin America were published posthumously in English as *The Motorcycle Diaries*. In them we see an enthusiastic young man, full of mirth and a desire for adventure. The casual style of his notes has the immediacy and freshness of someone who is discovering a different world. But Che also discovered that what he had seen in Argentina was true of the rest of the continent. And when he had to spend time in Miami waiting for a ride home, he saw how the gringo oppressed the poor in the United States. The contrast between rich and poor was astonishing and infuriating.

By 1953, now a doctor, he had left home again, this time never to return. At the end of that trip he·met Fidel Castro and joined his guerrilla force. They sailed from Mexico for Cuba in November 1956. The revolutionary war lasted two years, during which Che went from medical orderly to famed commandant. The chronicle of this struggle was published during his lifetime as *Reminiscences of the Cuban Revolutionary War*. In it he reveals his belief that popular forces can win a war against an army without having to wait for the right conditions: the insurrection itself will create them. This moving account reveals his humanity, his sense of humor, and his capacity for self-deprecation. He tells us that during an encounter with the enemy, he ran away so fast he would never be able to replicate such a feat.

Once in power in Cuba, Che wrote *Guerrilla Warfare*—a manual following in the footsteps of Chairman Mao and Vietnam's General Giap, made available free to guerrilla movements all over Latin America. Here Che expands on his theory that armed struggle could result in victory even against established, entrenched regimes armed with modern weaponry, and that guerrilla movements based in the jungles and mountains of a country could lead the people to freedom. I very much believed in all this at the time. Only, later, I discovered that Che Guevara had become criminal. I never understood why, but he committed murders and made bad policies, which damaged his own goals and the welfare of his country. At the time I met John, Che had just been killed in the Bolivian jungles, where I had also been, years ago.

So, in the beginning, John was not my type of man. Still, he was an appreciative listener, and the time we spent together flew by quickly. We talked for two hours and he ordered nothing. As I continued toward Stuttgart, he waved good-bye to me. What a friendly and typical American, I thought, but who knows if I will ever see him again. We did exchange addresses, but...

WINTER 1967, THE SECOND MEETING

Peter, my brother, had just left for Frankfurt, where he had studied sociology and was interviewing for a job at the university for a chair in futurology. Peter and I had many hot discussions about our aims in life and I—rather cruelly, but with much conviction—advised him to try something better than sociology or futurology. I said he was living in the clouds and had to come back to reality. He was dating Barbara, also a sociologist, and they were too high up in the skies for me and seemed to have lost touch with reality. However, I loved him. He was a Social Democrat, while I was a Christian Democrat. For many years, we had both participated in the Lutheran church, engaging in all kinds of youth activities. He had studied two years in Berkley, California, and analyzed everything in life, while I enjoyed life without analysis.

Anyway, Mutti, my mother, was at work that afternoon when the doorbell suddenly rang. As I opened the door, I couldn't believe it when I saw my friendly American visitor. He immediately explained that he really wanted to see me. He was in his late twenties and just said, "Hello, I'm happy I found you." I was startled and did not know what to say. "May I come in?" he continued.

"Of course," I said and guided him into our living room. "Can I offer you a glass of tea?" I continued, and we did some official chatting back and forth. It was early in the afternoon. He had come by train from Munich and stated that it was his first time in Stuttgart. "Well," I said, "I will show you the city." What else could I have offered?

We spent three hours on the streetcars and walking. I showed him our old castle and the Schlossplatz, and we strolled along the Königsstr. Sometimes he put his arm around me and I really liked that. Finally, we returned to my home in the late afternoon, and I told him that it would take him at least three hours by train to get back to Munich. My mother was due to come back a little later. When we walked up the stairs to our third floor, he drew me close and I felt him taking a deep breath. I liked him and felt an attraction, but was unsure about my feelings.

In the apartment, he asked, "Is your mommy back?"

"Not yet, but she may come at any moment."

Suddenly, he said, "Where is your room?" and I showed it to him. He took me in his strong arms and kissed me.

I was totally shocked but really touched by his embrace and told him, "John, please let us leave. I will take you back to the train station." He looked at me with his wonderful smile, and with love in his eyes said, "I am attracted to you and want to be with you." He did not wait for a response but kissed me again. I responded, feeling his desire, and was aware that I wanted him; I felt deeply touched by him. There was no way to resist him and we fell on the bed and were completely engaged with each other. He made me happier than I had ever felt before, and I forgot everything around me. We did not speak, and as I heard my mother moving outside, I touched him dearly and said, "Let us meet her."

Mutti had not realized that I was at home, and as she came out of the shower after work, I introduced John to her. She made no remark but found John a nice and polite gentleman. They later became good friends. I started to love this "Georgia boy," as he called himself. We found out that he had packed CARE packages in school from 1948 to 1952. I remembered those wonderful times in my childhood in Vienna, Austria, when we received CARE packages, supplied by the Marshall Plan, and filled with chocolate, raisins, and basic food items.

1967 AND 1968 IN GERMANY

Our young love began in Stuttgart. We only really met each other at the train station in Frankfurt, but slowly and deeply over the following year, our love grew. We met mostly in Munich but sometimes in Hamburg and also in Kiel and Stuttgart. We discovered each other as personalities very much engaged in different areas and totally immersed in our different professions. This left only a little time to develop our deep love and true friendship.

After starting my internship in Kiel in gynecology, I spent four months in Schwäbisch Gmünd (a town in Southern Germany), in internal medicine and three months in Stuttgart in general surgery.

Back in Kiel, I then had to gain ground through my continuous presence at the university hospital. The salary was minimal and the demands high, but this had priority in my life. I wanted to be a good and knowledgeable gynecologist and always thought that I had lost time due to my training to be a swimming star. I had participated in two Olympic Games with the West German National Team in Rome and Mexico City in the early 1960s.

I really had lost my heart to John and loved him. We spent a lot of our time together just listening to music, holding each other, and simply being together. A nice girl does not talk or write about these feelings; she just lives them. I found an apartment for John in München-Schwabing and loved to make it nice for him. He flew all around Europe and Germany with his job as manager of an investment company, and we met at many different places. I came from Schwäbisch Gmünd, Stuttgart, or Kiel by car, train, or plane. I found John a wonderful lover and true friend who would certainly one day marry a movie star or an actress. He was not very interested in my nightly duties, scientific studies, animal experiments, etc. We skied, sailed, traveled, cooked, and loved each other; neither of us thought about marriage at that time, and life between us was good and easy. There was never a cloud between us, and it seemed that we longed for each other. My eyes saw no other man in all these months who impressed me. I loved to listen to John's voice and felt wonderful in his arms. We mostly forgot the political ups and downs around us.

Politically, in those days, Germany had its eyes again on the mighty nation of America. We really did not like America earlier. The Vietnam War, which was still not finished, was very difficult to understand. Why did Americans have to fight in Vietnam, a country that had nothing to do with them? This question was difficult to answer.

One Friday afternoon in Kiel at around 5:00 in our Department of Obstetrics and Gynecology, the senior registrar suddenly decided to have an extensive ward round, which probably would have taken an hour or two. I was responsible there for the basic data of about thirty patients. I was just getting ready to leave the hospital to catch a 7:00 p.m. flight from Hamburg (an hour's drive from Kiel) to Munich. I told Dr. Reichert I had to leave. The late afternoon ward round had nothing to do with the special care of patients, but with his having been too busy in the daytime to have done it. He just said to me, "Dr. Mettler, if you leave now, on Monday we will fire you." Okay, I thought, I urgently have to see John and will face the situation on Monday. I flew to Munich, and in John's arms, I really forgot everything.

We spent nearly all our available hours at home and just left for a bite outside in some small Schwabing restaurant. I loved John too much and our time together was too precious.

Back in Kiel on Monday, Dr. Reichert suspended me from my duties, and in the afternoon I had a meeting with him and the director of the Gynecology Department. I stuck to my story that I'd had an important family obligation in Munich on Friday evening. The flight from Hamburg, which is a one-hour car trip from Kiel, takes one hour, and there was no later flight. I said that our duty on that Friday officially ended at 4:00 p.m. and that Dr. Reichert had decided to hold the ward round unexpectedly at 5:00 p.m. "If I had stayed, I would have missed my flight," and, I added softly, "meinen Liebling (my sweetheart)."

"Did she miss any of her official duties?" the director asked.

"No," answered Dr. Reichert. "She passed her information on to her friend Dr. Scholler but did not stay in the hospital herself for the ward rounds."

"Can you repeat your last words, Dr. Mettler?" the director asked. Blushing, I repeated that I would have missed my sweetheart.

"Who is this lucky man?" was his answer. He then turned to Dr. Reichert saying, "You better take care of the obstetrical ward as registrar this week, and we'll let Dr. Mettler take full care of her surgical ward with the help of another registrar who understands more about personal feelings." This was indeed not very nice to Dr. Reichert, but he really was a difficult man. Later on we often laughed about this event with Kurt Semm, the hospital director, who became my very good friend over the years. Dr. Reichert left the clinic after some months.

On one of the sunny but cold winter weekends in Munich, John and I went skiing on the Zugspitze in Garmisch, about an hour's drive south of Munich. My dear friend John wanted to go in his new black shoes, which of course got totally ruined in the snow before we ever reached the ski area. He was a funny and certainly sunny American, with a wonderful sense of humor. We never quarreled, were very busy, and loved to do things together. There was always music and happiness around us. I was successful in my medical work and had to study a lot. John was successful in his business; we wanted to have children together, but not yet.

JOHN'S THOUGHTS OF GERMANY IN 1967–68

▶ For the most part I found the German people wonderful. It was so hard to imagine we were at war twenty-three years earlier. This is the same country that produced giants such as Bach, Beethoven, Goethe, and Schiller—as well as Hitler and his ilk. Actually, Hitler was born in Austria. The longer I live, the more I realize how people all over the world are the same: they want security, love, independence, and happiness with their families. It is only the government and those in authority and their ever-ceasing push for power and control that causes the greatest problems, including misguided religious fanaticism and indoctrination. It has forever been thus. If there is a God, and I truly believe there is, He must truly be sad. Man, in fact, has been given free will.

Lisa's clinic was in Kiel about sixty miles north of Hamburg on the Baltic Sea. This lovely city of approximately 250,000 people was totally destroyed during World War II, as this was the location for the German Marine Center where all the submarines were built.

I came several times to her clinic in Kiel to see her. On one occasion we were in her room at the clinic where she was on duty. Lisa received an unexpected call for a delivery. She asked me if I would like to accompany her, and she would introduce me as the visiting doctor from America. I said, "Let's do it."

She proceeded to give me a white medical coat to put on, and as we walked down the stairs she told me not to say anything. I assured her that it would be my pleasure to be as quiet and unobtrusive as possible. As she worked on the actual delivery, I stood in somewhat of a military posture facing the wall with my hands behind my back. I knew then how great it was that God had given each of us different talents; mine certainly was not medical.

JOHN'S YOUTH IN THOMASVILLE, GEORGIA, USA

I was born on a plantation in the southern part of Georgia, which was comprised of approximately fourteen thousand acres overlooking a lovely, large lake and was called Lawridge Plantation. My father had been quite well-to-do, retiring at a relatively young age as president of the Law Brothers of the Royal Insurance Company out of Liverpool, England. As I understood it, his grandfather, Dr. John Stevens Law, established the first western branch in America, which became known as The Law Brothers. My father was the youngest president but had lost over a million dollars in the stock market crash of 1929, which was a considerable amount of money back then.

I was the youngest of four children. My sister, Elanne, with whom I am extremely close, threatened to hit me over the head with a hammer as a baby because I had usurped her position as the youngest. She was not allowed to be left alone with me. I had a brother and two sisters, and we all moved when I was six years old to a beautiful small town of Thomasville, which was twelve miles away. There were lovely historical plantations and piney oaks throughout the town. Thomasville had a population of some seventeen thousand and was known as the city of roses.

My father died at a young age, when I was only nine. I refused to go to the funeral. It was all too traumatic. I remember playing cowboys in an old building that had been demolished down on Broad Street the day of the funeral. I tried not to think of the event that was happening that day. I had many friends—both boys and girls—growing up. I was quite popular and excelled in nearly all sports, which was a very high priority in our small town. The competition with the teams of other nearby towns was intense. We usually won. My mother and my sister were my greatest cheerleaders and would attend nearly every game of whatever sport we were playing.

I remember the two things that I had a great passion to do as a profession for many years. One was to become a golf professional. I was quite accomplished at an early age. The other profession was the ministry. The element of God and the spiritual life and trying to find the meaning of why we are all here and what happens afterward were very important to me. From an extremely young age I always felt a close, personal connection to God. It has remained a cornerstone of my life. I was also very active in the Episcopal Church's youth group in Thomasville.

In my senior year of high school, I gave considerable thought toward college. The one place I decided on was Washington and Lee University in Virginia. This was one of the academically top-ranked schools in the country. George Washington had been president of the University and so had the great confederate general, Robert E. Lee, who is also buried on campus. I applied for admission but was heartbroken when the reply came back that my grades were not good enough! I wrote to the dean of admissions, Dean Frank Gilliam, and explained to him that although I had spent most of my energies on sports in high school, I would commit myself 110 percent to my academic studies, if only they would give me the opportunity! My intensity and commitment apparently made a difference. He wrote me back and basically said that with the attitude I conveyed, he would make an exception. I was elated! I didn't know at the time how little I was prepared for the studies and challenges ahead of me. I definitely got in over my head. I studied eight to ten hours a day after classes, and I came within one grade of failing out of school my first semester. I ended up graduating in the top third of my class my senior year. I had also been president of my freshman fraternity class, Phi Kappa Psi, as well as president of Scabbard and Blade, which was an honorary military fraternity on campus. I took ROTC and was commissioned as a second lieutenant upon graduation.

At the end of my sophomore year, I was chosen as one of fifty-four Americans as a Winant volunteer, named for John Winant, who had been the ambassador to the court of St James in London. I worked in Bethnal Green in London's East End, with the Cockneys, who were wonderful people. It was a most rewarding experience, and at the end of our summer work, which had been highly endorsed by the Royal Family, we Americans were invited to meet the Queen Mother at a party at her home at Clarence House. It was a most wonderful experience for a nineteen-year-old.

When I was commissioned as a second lieutenant, I was scheduled to spend only six months on active duty, and then I planned to marry my college sweetheart, Leslie, who went to Sweetbriar in Virginia.

Suddenly the Berlin Wall went up in 1961, and President Kennedy extended us officers to two years active duty. As life sometimes unfolds, Leslie and I parted ways, and I had an opportunity to serve my country in Germany. My first assignment was as platoon leader of the Fifty-fourth Infantry Armored Rifle Company in Heilbronn, Germany, and later I took over the position as commander of troops of the Fourth Armored Division, NCO Academy in Neu-Ulm. The academy was like the West Point in Germany for enlisted men who excelled in their position in the military. Neu-Ulm was separated from Ulm by the Danube and was the quaint German town where Einstein was born.

It was during this time in Neu-Ulm that I attended a very intensive military German language school for two weeks and developed basic conversational skills in German. Little did I know how well it would serve me and the many doors it would open, years later. This was also the year of the Cuban Missile Crisis, which was the standoff between the United States and Russia that could have easily developed into another World War. We were put on full alert in Germany. It was indeed a tense several days. Russia was at the height of its military power, but fortunately they diverted their ships from Cuba at the last minute. This was also the year that President John Kennedy was assassinated in Dallas, Texas. The entire world was in mourning.

JOHN'S VIEW ON LISA'S YOUTH

Lisa was born in Vienna, Austria and lived there until she was fourteen. At the age of five, her mother took her and her brother Peter and fled from what she thought would be a Russian invasion of Vienna. They lived in a small village in the mountains of Austria and her mother worked on a farm. Lisa would walk a mile to school every day. They finally returned to Vienna when she was seven.

Her brother, Peter, was two years younger, and they were very close. She often fixed him meals while their mother was working. The Russians had captured her father during World War II, when Lisa was only three years old. He was in a Russian prison camp for fifteen years. The family did not know if he was alive or dead during this time.

Growing up in Vienna, life was filled with interesting activities for Lisa. She learned fencing with her friend Gucki, loved school, where she excelled, and did endless mountain climbing. But her great love was swimming. She was in the Vienna swim club, where she swam competitively. I did not learn until much later that she swam on Germany's Olympic team in Rome. She won her race by three meters in the relay against the Dutch. To this day she is the happiest in the water, either swimming, which she does nearly every day, or sailing, which she could do forever, as any of her friends could attest.

She is a very accomplished sailor, and has her own forty-three foot sailboat in Kiel, Germany.

In Vienna, Lisa's mother made her learn to ice-skate and ice dance, which she hated. She was raised in the Lutheran church and always thought she would marry a Viennese man.

When she was fourteen, her mother moved the family to Stuttgart, Germany, where they lived with relatives. Her mother received a widow's compensation from the government and never received confirmation that Lisa's father was alive or dead.

The day Lisa left Vienna was a heartbreaking experience; she was forced to say good-bye to all her friends and enter into another world. The year was 1953. Stuttgart was very strange and hard for the whole family. In this area, people spoke a very harsh Schwäbisch German, which was hard to understand. They lived with Lisa's aunt and uncle. After a year, her mother was able to get her own private apartment, which was most welcome.

There in Stuttgart, Lisa also joined the swim club. They had great competition on the national and international level. She excelled in the breaststroke, and this became a very important part of her life. She was also actively involved with the Protestant church youth and later became an exchange student to Humboldt, Iowa in America. She found that she loved America and its unique ways, but she would always remain German and Viennese at heart.

When she was sixteen, her father returned from the prison camp in Russia. He returned first to Vienna and then came to Stuttgart. Unfortunately, Lisa's mother and father simply did not get along; certainly the prison camp had taken its toll on him. Her parents finally divorced before Lisa graduated from high school.

Peter and Lisa visited their father regularly. He remarried rather quickly and lived near Frankfurt. He was an engineer and built several of the wonderful autobahns (freeways) in Germany; one was the autobahn between Frankfurt and Heidelberg.

Lisa was growing up to become a lovely, athletic, and highly intelligent girl, and she was offered a scholarship for college in Iowa, but she chose to return to Germany and finish her high school there. She went on to become one of the top gynecologists in the world.

The early cold months of 1968 found Lisa and I totally in love. Our sexual intimacy and emotional bond unfolded beautifully, together with a spiritual connection and belief in God and mankind. Neither of us were great churchgoers, but when we did attend, it was meaningful and fulfilling. She would drive to Munich nearly every week in her little yellow Volkswagen bug, and we would immediately relish each other with kisses and closeness in my small apartment in Schwabing. Our side trips to Garmisch and Berchtesgarden and Chiemsee were happy and carefree. I was very involved with my successful investment work, and all was going well. My German was also improving. Lisa was extremely busy with her new medical career in Kiel. It was obvious she was made for the profession.

We often spoke of marriage, but we were a bit like explorers in the woods, not totally knowing our direction. There seemed to be no great urgency. Little did we know that dark clouds were gathering on the horizon.

1939–67/68 LISA'S STORY OF HER YOUTH AND ENTRY INTO LIFE'S ADVENTURES

▶▶I was born in Vienna, Austria in June of 1939, shortly before the outbreak of World War II in September of 1939. My father, a young German engineer, had just finished working on the construction of the autobahn between Stuttgart and Ulm in Southern Germany and was assigned to build the Vienna airport in Schwechat, outside of Vienna. He was a supporter of Hitler at the time, so he got a good job as an engineer and could provide well for his family. My brother Peter was born in Vienna in 1941. During the war, my father was transferred as an army major under Hitler to Bucharest, Romania. There, in 1945, he passed into Russian captivity, and we did not hear from him until 1959, when I graduated from high school in Stuttgart, Germany.

In 1945, in the face of the advancing Russian Army, my mother fled with us two children from Vienna to Tyrol. We were German citizens. In spite of Adolf Hitler's Austrian birth, the Austrians turned against the Germans after the end of World War II and claimed to have nothing to do with the Germans. Anyway, we found a home for two years with the family of a nice mountain farmer near Westerndorf in Tyrol, Austria. There I passed my first high school year and walked to school every day, one hour back and forth, with the son of the family whom they called Reiter-Seppl, which means "horseback-riding Seppl," because his father owned horses.

My mother worked for the farmer and received free board and lodging for all of us.

In 1947, two years after the end of World War II, we returned to Vienna. Westendorf later became a popular skiing village and many lovely hotels were built. We went back with my mother for a skiing vacation in 1980, thirty-three years after we had lived there, and found Reiter-Seppl was a hotel owner and the father of three children.

Back in Vienna in 1947, my mother got back our fancy, two-hundred-square-meter apartment. We lived rather narrowly in two rooms and survived by renting out the other rooms. I remember many of the families and individuals who rented our rooms, including an American soldier and lover of a Viennese girl, whom I called Uncle Jim. He sent us many CARE packages after his stay with us, which made us even happier. We never heard from our father.

I went to school—grade school, and later high school, and took swimming lessons in the Donau Club (the Danube Club). Interestingly, in spite of all the bombs that destroyed the area around the Danube channel in Vienna in 1944 and 1945, the Donau Club never got completely destroyed. This meant we could still practice our swimming there in large, wonderful swimming pools, one of which produced artificial waves every hour. I practiced every day and started to be a good swimmer. In the winter time, Mutti forced me to take ice-skating lessons which I never liked, but which gave me joy later in life when, a few years ago, I could make turns and lovely circles on an ice skating rink in the Red Square in Moscow.

On Sundays, as we were Protestant, we loved to go to a small Protestant church in the center of Vienna. The major religion in Vienna was Catholicism. Peter and I loved our church and all the activities there.

In 1954, my mother decided to seek repatriation, which would take us back to Germany where she would receive some financial compensation, since her husband was lost in the war. I thought her decision cruel, as I had such good friends in school and in my Danube swimming club in Vienna. We were repatriated to Stuttgart where we had some relatives who gave us a friendly reception. For me this was an extremely difficult time; I was furious and did not really understand my mother's decision. After six months we got our own apartment. My mother worked as a manager in a sports store and Peter and I had to look after ourselves during the day. I learned to cook for my younger brother and loved to do this. My specialty was Marillenknödel, but the recipe should remain a secret until I can cook it for you, dear reader.

Life was good to us. I continued with swimming, took part in some competitions, and joined the Schwimmerbund Schwaben. Peter and I were actively engaged in Youth for Christ and church life. I won several swimming races, and my trainer told my mother that I was talented. At that point, my mother decided to send me abroad for a year within the International Christian Youth Exchange (ICYE), which still operates today. I went for a year to a small town in Iowa, called Humboldt, into the corn state of the USA and the Royal Bennett family who accepted me as their exchange student with all their love. This family treated me like their own daughter, and I had a wonderful year in high school, in the family, and in their Methodist church.

I graduated from Humboldt High in 1958 after twelve years of schooling and had to do a thirteenth year in Germany to gain my Abitur, the German university-entrance diploma. Family life in Humboldt centered on church and school—it was a clean and Christian world. The Vietnam War had started in 1955, but in reality, it hardly reached the Midwest. The attempted uprising of Hungarian students in Budapest, an example of anxieties behind the iron curtain, went almost undetected there as well. Iowa in those years was totally quiet and peaceful.

Within the ICYE, we had high school refugees from Hungary who were then living in Vienna. One of the ICYE students who went to the United States was Gudrun Ensslin, a good guitar player. Even at her young age, she already posed many critical political questions. In the beginning she was only a rebellious student, but later, in the early 1970s, she became a member of the violent Red Army Faction (RAF) in her fight against the establishment. Gudrun Ensslin was one of the founders of the militant RAF whose activities ended in a terrible battle with many killings and bombings. She died in the Stammheim prison in Stuttgart in 1978.

I had also been active in marches against the establishment, but I soon came to realize how simple and shortsighted such activity was. My philosophy in life became realistic, and I understood that if you want to change something in life, you have to live it and convince others through your daily activities.

After my high school year in Iowa, I continued to serve the ICYE as an advisor for eight years and attended many evaluation camps in the USA and worldwide. I selected German high school students to participate in the exchange program and actively worked within the organization. We had many organizational meetings, and once a year we attended the ICYE evaluation and introduction meeting of all high school exchanges for that year. These were usually between five and seven hundred students from twenty-five to thirty-five countries.

ENCOUNTER WITH MARTIN LUTHER KING JR.

At one of these summer meetings in 1962 at Lake Okoboje, some of us tutors took an evening excursion into Old Town Chicago, walking along the streets, hand in hand with a Congolese minister friend. We got into a riot and were taken to jail. One of our invited speakers the next morning was Martin Luther King Jr. When he heard about our story he came himself—I remember very well—at ten o'clock in the morning with other friends of the ICYE program to secure our release from jail. That day we had such an interesting conversation with him. He apologized for his country and what had happened to us. What a great man, and how sad that he had to die so early.

As is well-known, the Reverend Martin Luther King Jr. was not only a clergyman but also an activist and the prominent leader in the African American civil rights movement in the 1960s. He was an iconic leader in the advancement of civil rights in the United States and around the world. In 1964, he became the youngest person to ever receive the Nobel Peace Prize. In 1968 he was tragically assassinated in Memphis, Tennessee at one of these summer meetings.

In my personal life, Sunday church services were soon integrated into the activities of the high school exchange program. I often had weekend swimming races and some conferences during medical school, but I attended Sunday church services as often as I could.

Many years later, during and after residency training, those weekend activities were filled with medical duties. Patient treatment and my total immersion in the development of assisted reproductive technologies (ART) and gynecological endoscopic surgery took up all my time. As much as I loved to go to Sunday church services, between 1981 and 1985 I spent many of my Sunday mornings in the hospital performing in-vitro fertilization (IVF) for our patients and loved every minute of it. This seemed to satisfy my church obligation during these years. Why? Well, the follicular puncture to aspirate a mature egg for in vitro fertilization has to be done when the eggs are ready, and this time varies from patient to patient and, of course, never respects a Sunday. The system then was not as organized as it is today. Now there are doctors and biologists who do this work regularly. At that time, patients depended on the few fanatical idealists who wanted to help their patients become pregnant and worked whenever it was necessary, even without payment. I will go into this again later.

LISA'S FINAL HIGH SCHOOL YEAR IN STUTTGART AND MEDICAL SCHOOL IN TÜBINGEN, GERMANY

My final high school year was in Stuttgart, Germany, 1958–1959. In Germany, we have thirteen years of schooling, counting grade school and high school. We have one more year than the rest of the world, although this is now gradually changing. The year was difficult, but finally I graduated from the humanistic Hölderlin gymnasium. I continued with my swimming training, races, and youth life within the church. To earn some money, I taught German lessons to American soldiers stationed outside of Stuttgart in the Kelly Barracks. Little did I know that one day I would fall in love with an American.

In 1959 I was selected to be one of the four delegates of the Christian Youth of Germany for the World Council of Churches meeting in Uppsala, Sweden. These World Council meetings were wonderful and gave us a chance to exchange our ideas of faith and convictions of life with wonderful young people from around the world.

Also in 1959, I started my medical studies in Tübingen, near Stuttgart. It was the year my father returned from Russian captivity and rejoined the family in Stuttgart. We were all very happy, but we did not live affluently. After his long term of imprisonment, my father wished to live a richer, more expensive life. He also came back with tuberculosis. My mother worked hard but wasn't yet able to buy a car. Dad's desire to live an exuberant life after Russian captivity was also understandable. Mom had to work hard just to send us to school, and they had many long discussions about this. The marriage didn't work out and during a period of convalescence in the Black Forest, he decided to marry a rich lady, although my mother had waited for him all these years. We, as children, tried to understand and did understand. His second marriage did not last very long. Next he married an actress, a love of his younger years. I never thought that this might happen to me. His third marriage also ended unhappily, due to some unpleasant misunderstandings with his third wife, Jenny. My mother took care of my father until he died at the age of ninety. She later helped me enormously with my children, as I continued with my medical work after giving birth and only took short periods of motherhood leave. My mother lived to be ninety-seven.

1960 OLYMPICS IN ROME, ITALY

In 1959 and 1960, during my first years of medical school in Tübingen, I continued to swim and train every day. My strength was the one-hundred-meter and two-hundred-meter breaststroke. I was totally surprised when I heard that I had qualified for the Olympic swimming team and was invited to join the West German team in Rome. I swam in the two-hundred-meter breaststroke relay. We lost the bronze medal by ten centimeters to the Dutch team. Pierre de Coubertin, the founder of the Olympic Games, said, "To have been a participant is the only thing that counts."

The entire Olympic experience was fantastic. It was overwhelming to be part of the Opening Ceremony and to march with our team through the stadium with the world looking on. We giggled and laughed a lot. I must say I did not take it as seriously as maybe I be should have.

I met very many interesting and dedicated athletes. Gucki, my Viennese friend was a member of the Austrian floret fencing team, and we both enjoyed the hospitality given to us as Olympic team members and established our extra-team life. Despite our daily training schedule, we had many free hours and loved to escape with our Italian friends on their Vespas, which were hired for the transport of the athletes, to swim at Rome's beaches. It was a beautiful summer, and we had fun. We were out in the evenings, but I do remember that we drank no alcohol. Little did we understand that this was not allowed.

We had already swum three heats and were hoping to reach the final. To my great surprise, my trainer told me one day that we had reached the final.

"Tomorrow morning you'll swim against Eva in the two-hundred-meter breaststroke and whoever wins will swim in the medley relay final tomorrow afternoon," he said. I beat Eva and had the honor of representing the West German swimming team in the hundred-meter medley relay. There was also an East German team—the reunification of Germany didn't take place until 1989.

The day of the race I was extremely excited, yet also felt a strange calm. As I stood there at the side of the huge Olympic pool, memories flashed through my mind of the hours, months, and years I had trained for this, without any expectation of ever making it, and yet here I was, minutes away from the greatest swimming competition of my life. My women competitors were all lined up, and we quickly exchanged glances. I tried to smile at them, but everyone was too focused and serious about what lay ahead to smile back. I understood. The referee started the count and the whistle blew. The crowd in the stands was going wild, but it was all beyond me. I focused on what was at hand like never before in my life. The relay started with the butterfly swimmer, followed by the backstroke; I was the third swimmer in the breaststroke. As I entered the water, I felt a very strange sensation. It was the only time in my life I truly felt I was one with the water. I was vaguely aware of the girls on each side of me, but I was exploding with adrenalin, and the girls became a blur. As we came to the end of the race, I felt my hand slam into the poolside. I immediately looked around; to my astonishment, I had won by three meters. Anna, our last swimmer, jumped in as soon as I touched the wall and gave her very best in the freestyle, but was only able to finish fourth, giving our West German team fourth position overall.

We cried and laughed, and all the tension disappeared. When the Dutch anthem was sung at the winners' ceremony for the bronze medal, we had tears in our eyes, embraced each other, and swore eternal friendship. Emotions were high; the world belonged to us. Luckily, our good friends in the West German rowing team won a gold medal. With joy, we joined in singing the West German anthem, which at that time was part of Beethoven's *Seventh Symphony* as they went on stage to receive the Gold Medal: "Freude Schoener Goetterfunke Tochter aus Illision." Their whole team came from Kiel, which became my home five years later.

Swimming gave me a lot, and I continued with competitions for a while. I was still a member of the West German Olympic team four years later and went to Tokyo but did not get to swim. During the 1972 Munich Summer Olympics, I served as a medical doctor at the sailing events in Kiel. At that time I was already in gynecological residency training in Kiel. Later, I served for a while on the German Olympic Committee. We lost the bid for the 2012 Summer Olympics to London but are now hoping to win the 2018 Winter Olympics for Germany. In 1936, the Summer Olympics were held in Berlin, with the sailing events in Kiel, but Germany has never been the site of the Winter Olympics. Maybe we'll have a chance one day.

LOVING LISA AND "BUSINESS CONFLICTS"

▶ On one of her weekend trips from Kiel to Munich on a beautiful warm Friday night, I picked Lisa up at the train station. It was about 7:00. I waited on the platform as everyone got off; at first I thought my darling had missed the train, for she was literally the last one off. Even though she was far away, I knew that energetic walk with blond hair blowing in the wind; she was briskly rolling a small suitcase behind her. As she came closer, her beautiful smile said it all—there was such love in her eyes, and I knew she saw the love in my eyes, too. We embraced, and I gave her a small kiss on her beautiful mouth. My hand "accidentally" brushed across the upper portion of her blouse and she, in pretended anger, said, "You are so rude."

"I know," I replied. "Isn't it wonderful?" I then asked her, "Are you hungry, my love, or do you want to go back to our little apartment?"

"Let's go to the apartment." She smiled. "I want to talk to you for a while." I knew what "talking" meant, and I felt excitedly the same.

"Fine," I replied. "I have a lot to say to you as well." She smiled knowingly.

The apartment was a twenty-minute taxi ride from the station. As we went up the elevator in Enhubertstr, number six, we couldn't stop kissing. As I opened the door, Lisa fell into my arms, and we smothered each other with our mouths.

"Please come to bed," I said. "I have a lot to tell you."

"And I you," she replied, as she quickly removed her black shirt.

"You are so beautiful, my baby, with your sexy, athletic legs—the legs of a swimmer." We couldn't stop exploring each other with our hands and every part of our bodies. I had lit a small candle, and our shadows reflected on the wall. It was very provocative. When I touched her legs, she was wonderfully responsive and pulled me lovingly inside her. "I do love you, my Lisa. Yes, you are sexy as hell, but this closeness is much deeper and touches deep, deep within my heart or soul or someplace."

"I know," she replied. "My feelings are so strong for you, my John." We made beautiful love, and I was thrilled at her orgasms. We finally fell asleep for a short time. As we opened our eyes, I glanced at the clock. It was 10:30 p.m.

"Darling, I've enjoyed so much our 'conversation,'" I whispered. "Shall we have a small dinner at our nearby restaurant?"

"Yes, my love, I would like that," she whispered. We could hear police sirens in the distance.

As I had mentioned, the international investment company for whom I worked had its headquarters in Los Angeles. Volker became one of my best friends in the Munich office. He was an accomplished attorney and spoke perfect English. His primary responsibility was to legally guide us through the maze of German requirements in selling our funds and creating new funds. We would often have lunch together at a nearby restaurant in Schwabing and talk over all that was happening with our business. Volker was a tall, slender man who always seemed very serious, especially when he pulled his glasses down over his nose when speaking to you like an attorney. But, at the same time, he had a ready smile and an easy laugh; he seemed to share my sense of humor. We liked each other and developed a real trust for one another. As you may know, the Germans are very slow in developing relationships, but when they do, it is usually for life. It was a special moment when Volker finally said to me, "Johann, bitte sag zu mir Du und nicht Sie (Please speak to me with the familiar form of 'you' and no longer the formal 'Sie')." We drank to Freundschaft (friendship), and, as the months passed, our friendship grew.

In due time, we both became painfully aware that things did not appear to be happening properly with the head person in the office. Let's call this individual Eduardo for the sake of hiding this person's identity. He was a most charming individual from Ecuador, but neither Volker nor I felt his methods and business conduct with our trusted German clients was appropriate. Actually, he was hurting our reputation and the reputation of our company in Los Angeles. We felt very trapped and didn't know exactly what to do. The value of our domestic and international stock price was also dropping, as was the overall New York Stock Exchange.

Volker had met the head people in Los Angeles only a couple of times, and I had spent only three weeks in Los Angeles before being sent to Munich. So our contracts and relationships there were not strong. We had recently created a new international mutual fund for Europe, and I had received over one million dollars in stock options. Obviously, I had an incentive to try to resolve the developing mistrust that was growing with our German clients.

I often spoke to Lisa about this dilemma and told her I was not sure how to handle it. Our German clients were constantly asking me pointed and embarrassing questions about our "procedures." My dear Lisa was obviously not familiar with the investment business and its procedures, but she did tell me that I appeared much more impressive to the German people than did Eduardo. She never liked him. I am sure her opinion was not totally unbiased. Over the years, I have come to highly value the feelings and intuitions of women. The phrase "women's intuition" exists for a reason.

Several weeks after I arrived in Munich, I decided to establish my official residence in Brussels for tax purposes. My financial compensation was significant enough to compel me to legally shelter as much as I could from U.S. taxes. Brussels, considered the "office window" of Europe, was ideal. Through a capable attorney there, I rented a one-bedroom apartment as my official residence. Brussels is a lovely place with very nice people and a wonderful history.

I continued my extensive travels from Munich to Düsseldorf and Köln every week, meeting with German banks and giving one- or two-hour presentations in German to our mutual fund dealers. Our greatest competition was IOS (Investment Overseas Services). We were the new kid on the block, but our fund performance was incredibly profitable for our investors and made the selling of shares relatively easy.

There was great demand from the banks and large investment houses, as well as from wealthy individuals. Our record and reputation was one of the best in the United States, and everyone, it seemed, wanted a piece of it. All my life I had taken great pride in the company or product I represented. Certainly I had made my share of mistakes, but my clients trusted my integrity. This is why I literally had so many sleepless nights over the clouds and conditions that were taking place in our office. My clients wanted answers about why their shares were dropping and the lack of communications and forthrightness from our Munich office. I found myself sidestepping many questions and dancing around the issues. I tried to reassure my clients that answers would be forthcoming as soon as I had them. Eduardo, however, refused to answer many questions and always tried to put a positive spin on what were serious issues; it was the Band-Aid approach relating to serious wounds. Eduardo became very defensive and authoritarian when I approached him on these issues; I think that's how many problem issues were handled in South America. Volker and I found ourselves rather isolated and totally frustrated in this box of secrecy. The German clients totally trusted Volker, the attorney, and were amazed they were not getting facts from him. The situation was becoming very explosive.

The one ray of sunshine in my life at this time was my Lisa. The love we had was special and the friendship that we shared was genuine and real. I loved talking with her, even though I knew my repetition of my problems was burdensome. She never tired of listening and giving me her thoughts, which I valued.

One cold and snowy weekend when she flew down to Munich, I said, "Let's get away to Garmisch," which was a lovely, quaint ski town in the Alps, only seventy-five miles from Munich.

She responded, "I would love to ski on the Zugspitze and stay for two nights." It was a great relief to be on the train with her and to forget, if only briefly, the heavy problems of business and Eduardo. I had lost respect for Eduardo and was starting to greatly dislike him.

As the train sped further south, snowflakes gently hit the windows. It was quite beautiful, as was my lovely darling beside me. "You make me happy," I whispered as I gave a little kiss on the check.

"I am glad," she said. "You know how you make me feel." We arrived in Garmisch around 2:00 p.m. We rented some skis and were on the slopes by three. The sun was still shining, and we had a good three hours left of daylight. We took the lift close to the top of the Zugspitze and timed our jump off at the appropriate moment. We pulled our goggles down, and away we went.

Lisa skied so beautifully and athletically. Her sexy derriere swayed back and forth in her tight black ski pants as we descended the slopes. By comparison, my level of skiing was not nearly as good, but it was still more than adequate. The Germans were born on skis and they were as aggressive on the slopes as they were driving their cars. There was one very arrogant German who suddenly crossed my path, missing me by about five feet. This show-off got a very dirty look from me and a few choice words in German; I found myself holding back my temper.

"So ist das leben," I kept telling myself. Such is life. I was too happy with my Lisa to really let childish showboating upset me. We made the run two more times. She would always have to wait for me at the bottom, and when I finally arrived she would clap her hands in mock celebration. "Okay—that's enough," I said. "Let's go for some beer and hot wine at the Gaststube on the hillside over there." The combination of the snowy cold air and the dripping sweat from our runs was exhilarating as we stood by the open fire. I loved my Lisa.

We had found a cozy room in a small, charming hotel in the middle of Garmisch. Our balcony overlooked the street

below, and we could see sleighs drawn by horses quietly passing by; it was something out of a storybook, but it happened to be true. "Let's have a nice warm shower together," she whispered.

"Wonderful," I responded. The water felt totally refreshing after our skiing. We gently rubbed each other with soap and let the warm water splash us clean. Lisa loved long showers and baths. We then fell into bed and made beautiful love. We fell asleep for an hour and were awakened by some happy people singing down below. We decided to stay at the hotel for dinner, and our German waitress was attractive and attentive. It was the first time I had ever had steak tartare; it was made to perfection and accompanied by a glass of red wine. We were very, very happy and did not want this time to end.

It was a quiet train ride back to Munich. Neither of us said much. We felt close, but there was also an air of apprehension due to the problems that still lay unsolved at my office. Lisa could pick up vibrations so easily. That night I took her to the airport and we spoke of our next meeting.

Monday morning came bright and early with sirens in the distance. I dressed in coat and tie and made my way to the office. Eduardo had gone to London for a few days and was not yet back.

Suddenly, the front door opened abruptly and Eduardo hurried in with suitcase in hand. We exchanged cool greetings, and Rosemary, our dear secretary, immediately handed him a cup of tea. "Volker," he yelled, "Go get me two packs of cigarettes from the store—you know the kind." It was embarrassing to me how he treated a respected attorney and my friend like some houseboy.

I said to him, "Why don't you get your own cigarettes, Eduardo? Don't you think Volker has more important things to do?" He glared at me.

"John, can we talk for a minute in my office?" he asked. Sure, I replied. He closed the door and the two of us sat facing each other across the desk. "John, I get the feeling something is bothering you."

"There definitely is," I replied. "Our fund representatives and investors are not getting straight and clear answers about our procedures and the dropping price in our fund. There are millions of dollars at stake here, and we seem to be dancing around their questions and real concerns. It makes all of us look bad. Whatever the problems are, both here and back in LA, let's be straightforward and honest with them."

There was a knock on the door and Volker entered with cigarettes in hand. "That will be all, Volker," Eduardo dismissed him. Eduardo was a short man as he leaned back in his chair; his feet came off the floor. It was a bit comical. He slowly lit a cigarette and said, "The hell with the fund reps and banks and investors. They are lucky to have us and lucky to have a place to put their money. They have never seen returns like we've provided over the past two years! They are like little children and need to be treated as such. Just tell them this is temporary. The prices will go back up and leave the company procedures to us; they don't need to know." Eduardo's answers were totally unacceptable and sickening.

"I've got to catch a plane to Düsseldorf for a talk," I said as I got up and walked out. The air between us could have been cut with a knife, and he knew it.

The next week everything deteriorated. I knew things were not right, but I was unsure of how to handle it. Selfishly, I had a million dollars at stake, and at the same time I could see and feel our company's reputation plummeting. The secrecy that pervaded the office was terrible. Eduardo wanted to keep things quiet with total control, South American style. "Divide and conquer" seemed to be his motto. None of us felt free to discuss things openly anymore. What used to be an atmosphere of happy, friendly, and open office meetings had become one-man rule behind closed doors.

About a week later, I awoke in the middle of the night, and the decisions were very clear to me. Being the only American in the German office, I had to let the home office know in Los Angeles. I felt compelled to explain as best I could the atmosphere and mistrust that had developed here. They needed to know that not only had morale become a problem within the office, but also that our banks and investors deeply mistrusted our business practices and Eduardo.

When I made that important call to Los Angeles, I was amazed to hear that in the previous days our head people had resigned and were gone. The two people I had the most contact with were no longer there. Jim, who I spoke with and knew casually, was amazed that we had not been notified in the Munich office of the changes. I did not realize it at the time, but Eduardo had Jim under his thumb, and Jim was the main contact person for the Munich office. As I tried to explain our circumstances, Jim replied, "I can't be bothered with that right now, John. I have to speak with Eduardo." It became clear to me that the real strength in our home office was no longer there, and the new attitude seemed to be one of basic survival. In the meantime, share prices continued to drop. I had to talk with Lisa.

We arranged to meet at the Hotel Atlantic on the Alster in Hamburg. I told her as best I could all that was happening and what I was feeling. I felt I could not continue working under those corrupt circumstances. She seemed to understand and asked about us. "You know I love you, my Lisa, and I know you love me, but the time is not right for either of us right now. I am in the midst of a huge upheaval, and you are just beginning what will probably be a magnificent medical career. I must go back to the U.S. and see what I can sort out. We have to take one step at a time right now and sadly that step means I will have to leave for a while."

"I understand," she whispered, with tears in her eyes.

It was a sad farewell when I told Volker I had to go back to LA and see if I could possibly sort out what was really happening at the home office. He told me, emotionally, "Johann, I can understand what you are doing, but you are the one person representing the U.S. that the people not only like but trust over here. I don't know how it will be taken when you leave. The fact of the matter is I may not be far behind. The working conditions here with Eduardo are intolerable. You and I will always remain friends."

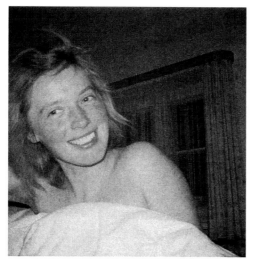

My darling Lisa and I agreed to meet one last time in Hamburg, and from there I would fly back to Los Angeles. We spent a beautiful last night together filled with love and passion and sadness. It's interesting how life causes us not to fully appreciate something or someone until we have lost it. Somehow we both felt that one day we would meet again. We had spoken of marriage, but things all around us were so unsettled, and there was such a personal upheaval on my part, that we made what we both thought a sad but temporary good-bye. We never broke up; we just said good-bye. I gave her my red and black blanket to keep.

JOHN'S NEW PROFESSIONAL AND PERSONAL LIFE IN THE UNITED STATES AFTER 1968

It was a typical rainy German morning as my plane roared down the runway, headed for LA. It was with a very heavy and sad heart that I leaned back in the seat and looked out the window at the gray and rainy sky. What in the world was I doing leaving Lisa, who was truly the love of my life? Hopefully it would not be for long.

When I got back to the home office in LA, I asked to speak directly to the president, Doug Becher. I explained to him all that was happening in Germany and the deteriorating trust and morale of our investors, fund reps, banks, and entire office personnel. He acknowledged what I was explaining and replied, "I know Elwin"—he only knew me as Elwin—"I am aware of many of the problems you speak of. I got a feeling about this the last time your friend Mark was over in Germany; unfortunately he is no longer with us. We are coping with many huge problems right now domestically. The German situation has to be put on the back burner at this time."

"I understand," I replied. "Thank you very much for spending the time. I hope you know I have great respect for you."

"And I you, Elwin. I've heard many good things about you and your work. I hope you will stay with us."

It was with a heavy heart that I left the office. My interest was working internationally in Germany and not domestically in the United States, but I knew it was an untenable situation. I felt in the midst of no-man's-land. It was time to leave and make a total change in my life. I thought of Lisa and silently sent her my love.

My decision to leave cost me my job and one million dollars in stock options. Even though I had the highest producing area in all of Europe, I was out! This was a devastating time for me, and my anger and sense of total injustice was at a fever-pitch level. All was gone and my hopes were dashed in a single moment!

I was literally a refugee and could not stay in the United States for a period of six months due to the fact that I had established my residence in Brussels for tax purposes, and those were the laws required by the United States. This truly was one of the darkest periods in my life. I moved temporarily to Vancouver, British Columbia, and found simple jobs to tide me over since I did not have a Canadian work permit. I had also lost a substantial amount of money in the plummeting value of our stock over the past year. I tried as best I could to appreciate the physical beauty and good things all around me. After all, I still had my health and life was still ahead of me.

Finally, in 1970, I was able to return to the United States. My position with Paine–Webber stock brokerage in Santa Monica was still available, but I wanted to make a change in my life and change in cities. After many visits between San Francisco and La Jolla, I finally decided on the beautiful seaside and quaint village of La Jolla, which was the jewel of San Diego.

I loved the proximity to Mexico, only twenty-five miles south, and the near-perfect climate year round. There was also the geographic diversity of ocean, mountains, and desert—all within two hours. I returned to what I knew, which was the stock brokerage business. I joined a very highly respected local San Diego firm and many of my special clients from Santa Monica came with me once they were notified I was back in the business.

I thought of Lisa and thought perhaps one day the right time would bring us back together again. I challenged the old saying, "Absence makes the heart grow fonder."

My brokerage business was going well, with the normal ups and downs and highs and lows that are so characteristic of the business. After about four months with the company, I received a special recognition for having opened more new accounts in one month than anyone in the history of the company. That also was the lifeblood of the brokerage business.

I had a beautiful office in La Jolla overlooking the Pacific and was in by 6:30 a.m. for the opening bell of the New York Stock Exchange. I would often take a twenty-minute break during the market session and walk to the ocean to quiet my nerves and thoughts.

As I looked across the vastness of the ocean, I felt wonderful peace and serenity. I wondered what Lisa was doing and how her medical career was progressing. I was sure she was doing well. I wondered if she was thinking of me.

As the months and years passed, I began to grow tired of the monotony of the market and the emotional roller coaster ride of the highs and lows of the stock brokerage business. I especially was growing tired of how microscopic my world had become. My life was eating and sleeping and breathing the brokerage business. When my clients' investments were going up, I felt pure joy and a real rush. When they were going down, I felt responsible and a sense of urgency. After three years, I realized that I wanted more of life, and I wanted to experience a broader and less hectic day in, day out existence. I had been very blessed in all that I had received and experienced because of the brokerage business, both in Santa Monica and La Jolla. It was also the brokerage business that had given me my wonderful experiences in Germany and Lisa. I would always love her.

I had a very friendly and cordial parting of the ways with the La Jolla company and decided to take a sabbatical for a couple of months and reevaluate my life and direction. It seemed that my life was meant to be a series of meaningful, yet different, endeavors. There were so many things in life that interested me and fortunately, so far, I felt that I had excelled in nearly everything in which I had become involved.

There were many people through the years, for whom I had a great deal of respect, who told me that I would be a natural in the real estate business. They were of the opinion that my ability with people and my negotiating skills would serve me very well in that profession. I had been too involved with my stocks to really consider real estate. I looked around at the most beautiful, and still relatively undiscovered, places in La Jolla, and I knew people from all over the world would be moving here for the beauty and peace and incredible climate, and that surely real estate values would increase. It's funny how life propels one in a given direction at different times. Sometimes not being happy or fulfilled in one's work can be a great blessing in that it causes a change of direction. I knew I would always have a love for stocks, but it was more on a personal basis and did not involve other people or businesses. In many ways I suppose I am a loner, or I certainly value my privacy and independence even though I love people and love being with them. They say that one must be happy in oneself before one can ever really be happy or of value to others.

I awoke one summer morning at about 4 a.m., and decided clearly that I would go into the real estate profession. I had always wanted to help people and what could be better than assisting them with one of their most significant purchases in life, their home? It also could also pay extremely well if one was good at it. I decided to go with what I thought was one of the best companies in the business, Coldwell Banker.

Ironically their beautiful office was located only half a block away from my previous brokerage office on Prospect Street. I called and requested an interview with the manager, Rob Jackson, and we had a very nice meeting. Much to my surprise at the end of our meeting he politely told me that even though I had an impressive resume, there was no room for anyone else in the office at this time, and besides, they only accepted agents who had previous experience in real estate. I looked at him intensely and said, "Rob, perhaps I did not adequately explain myself. I want to work here and with no other company, and I can assure you that if you will make an exception, you will not regret it!" I meant this sincerely, and it must have resonated with him.

"All right, Elwin," he said. "We'll give it a try." I sold my first property five days later.

There was so much for me to learn, but I seemed to take to this new work naturally. I especially enjoyed the great satisfaction of really helping people and experiencing their sincere appreciation. I enjoyed the psychology, and I especially enjoyed the negotiations. I quickly developed a good reputation and received wonderful referrals from satisfied clients.

I remember one transaction where I was representing a client on a particular property in La Jolla. It was what was called a really hot property and had four different offers to purchase at the same time. There were other full-price offers from other agents, and possibly offers above the asking price with a substantial deposit. I explained this to my client and gave him some specific advice, which he followed. The listing agent representing the seller told me, as one of the four agents with offers, that we could all meet at the seller's home and personally present our offers. This process is done so differently today; a lot has been lost, in my opinion. We all met at the property at 8:00 on a Friday evening. I walked in and three other highly qualified agents were sitting there waiting to present their offers. Some were, in fact, in excess of the listing price. We all exchanged pleasantries and I proceeded to explain to the listing agent that we have a full-price offer and the property has already been sold to us.

"But there are other offers higher than your client's," she replied.

"Your seller has agreed to sell his home at a specific price and under certain terms and conditions. We have totally accepted that offer to sell at that price and those specified terms and conditions with no contingencies whatsoever, and therefore that constitutes a binding agreement. It's as simple as that; a contract has been formed!" I responded. It was a totally unique approach, and we ended up with the property in spite of higher offers. I later discovered that my position and reasoning could certainly have been legally challenged, but it never was! My client was elated.

JOHN'S FAMILY LIFE, ESTABLISHING "LAW & ASSOCIATES" 1972–2009

As life went on, I met a wonderful woman, Charlotte, from the Boston area. She was highly intelligent and had a wonderful heart and feelings. After a period of time, we decided to marry. It all seemed to just fall into place, and she was extremely helpful and supportive in my work. I knew I would never forget Lisa, but it just seemed not to be our fate. I always kept her address at the Frauenklinik in Kiel, Germany. Charlotte and I later had two wonderful children, Todd and Dana, with whom I have an incredible relationship to this day. They both live in San Diego very close to me. We are the best of friends, along with dear Sarah, Todd's wife and Aramis, who is a wonderful husband to my Dana. We all do many things together. I am very blessed.

My work with Coldwell Banker continued to go well. After three years I got my broker's license and decided to establish my own company, Law & Associates. I loved the independence of being my own boss and making my own decisions and mistakes.

La Jolla has its own organization of real estate agents and brokers, the Real Estate Broker's Association of La Jolla, also known as REBA. This truly is one of the finest and one of the most professional and ethical real estate organizations in the country, and it enjoys a wonderful reputation. The agents and brokers there are truly some of the finest people I have ever met, and we enjoy a very close kind of bond and working relationship.

In 1978 I was elected Chief Financial officer of REBA and produced the very first dividends ever paid to the members. In 1979 I was extremely honored to be elected president. It was also a very tumultuous time for the organization thanks to the introduction of the computer, which changed the nature of the business. In the old system, we updated our listings by hand, which made our business in La Jolla very exclusive. There were two very strong and loyal groups—those who wanted to keep the old system, which had been in effect since the founding of REBA, and the new school who wanted to expand and modernize via the computer. There were very turbulent waters, and we had to cross them without tearing our organization apart. Fortunately, we crossed the waters successfully and eventually went the route of computerization, which opened up REBA throughout San Diego County.

At this time, Jimmy Carter was president, and interest rates for real estate were an exorbitant 22 and 23 percent. Loans were extremely difficult to obtain and the use of sophisticated wrap-around or all-inclusive trust deeds were rampant. I was fortunate that even during these difficult times my business prospered. I almost felt that I did better in bad times than good times. During this time, the country also experienced the tragic and nationally embarrassing Iran Hostage Crisis. In my opinion, Carter was one of the most moral presidents we have ever had, but he was also one of the worst and most inept Presidents we have ever had, next to our present administration.

This period was also marked by hyperinflation, and the value of the three homes I owned in La Jolla increased substantially.

I also took a flyer and speculated in the gold and silver commodity market. This was when the Hunt Brothers out of Texas were thought to have had a corner on the silver market. I took a $15,000 investment and turned it into $180,000 in six weeks. I lost $60,000 in one hour when silver unfortunately started crashing, and I got out. It was an intoxicating ride. Charlotte and I enjoyed the ability and comfort of having wonderful Mexican live-in domestic workers for a number of years; they were very helpful in the caring and raising of Dana and Todd. Life was good. Many times as I took private walks at La Jolla Shores beach, I would think of Lisa and wondered what her life was like. How strange the course of events is in each of our lives. One must believe that there is a reason things happen the way they do, even though we certainly do not understand why at the time. I wondered if Lisa still had my red and black blanket. Would we ever meet again? I sometimes thought of writing and asking about her life and how things were, but there was something inside of me that would rather not know. I suppose I wanted to be left with our own special memories that only we had shared.

The years passed, and Todd and Dana were growing up so nicely. I got them both into sports at an early age. Dana excelled at jump rope and was on a special school team. She performed beautifully for audiences, including a Russian team. Todd excelled at every sport he ever attempted—a true natural athlete.

Somehow, over the years, Charlotte and I found ourselves drifting apart. We had very different interests and goals, and these became great differences between us. Eventually in 1990 we decided to divorce, but we hoped to remain friends and to respect the years we had together. We totally agreed never to speak badly about one another to our children, whom we both loved with all our hearts. Everyone seemed to adjust as well as could be expected. It probably will go down as one of the friendliest divorces in history. We would get together for holidays and birthdays and celebrate with great care in our hearts. We both wanted the very best for Dana and Todd, and fortunately and thankfully, we succeeded.

In 2000, Charlotte moved back to Boston to care for her elderly parents who very much needed her. She would come back to La Jolla every Christmas and birthday. The children would also visit in Boston once or twice a year and they would constantly stay in touch by phone. One never marries with the idea of divorce, but either you grow together through the years or you grow apart, at which point we all make our personal decisions.

I had my work and many friends throughout the years. It was amazing how many clients had become my best friends. I loved and valued being an integral part of Todd and Dana's lives and development.

Through the years I had several relationships, a couple rather serious, but I never felt a connection that would induce me to marry again. Dana would often ask, "Dad, would you ever get married again?" I would answer that I would love to marry again if I should ever find a woman that touched me in that way, and if that never happened, that would be okay too. I figured if God or the universe should have that in store, I would welcome it. Qué será será, as they say. Obviously, I was not totally fulfilled in my life. I felt I had so much love to give to the right woman.

LISA'S MEDICAL STUDIES AND SPECIALIZATION IN OBSTETRICS AND GYNECOLOGY

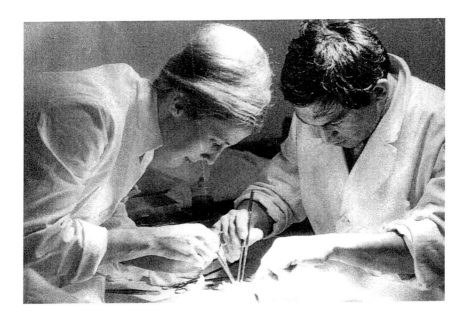

▶▶ My medical studies took place in Tübingen, Vienna and finally in Kiel. In 1965 I graduated from medical school in Kiel. Clinical and scientific studies including the PhD thesis went hand in hand and kept me busy.

In 1966 and 1967 I worked in a jungle hospital, Amazon Hospital Albert Schweitzer in Peru.

When I met John in 1967, I had just settled back in Germany and was starting my specialization in obstetrics and gynecology.

After having finished some practical general surgical training in Stuttgart and Schwäbisch Gmünd, I decided to start my academic life at Kiel University in 1968.

John and I had a great year of love and joy together in 1967–68. For me he was the sunny pole in a life filled with sweet music, love, and care.

During this time, there was a student uprising in Germany against the establishment and against the media, especially publications from the Axel Springer publishing house. The students wanted a move toward social democracy, as practiced by Konrad Adenauer after World War II. A wave of protests swept Germany that resulted in the death of the student Benno Ohnesorg in 1967. The so-called '68 student revolution in Germany and the RAF (Rote Armee Fraktion) published books on the "armed battle." At Easter 1968 a young German neo-nationalist attempted to assassinate the Marxist student leader Rudi Dutschke (1940–79) in Berlin. This led to further student revolt against the post-war establishment in Germany. Rudi Dutschke was seriously injured and this finished his political career.

My co-high school exchange with the International Christian Youth Exchange in the USA was Gudrun Ensslin, who later joined the RAF and burned down warehouses. The RAF, in its early stages commonly known as the Baader-Meinhof group, was engaged in armed resistance to the state and was responsible for the deaths of many political figures in the 1970s. I sympathized with this leftist movement in the beginning, but I also had my own line of thinking and criticized them. The son of my professor of internal medicine, Thomas Weissbecker, had also joined the RAF movement and was killed in 1972.

My dear, sunny American friend John was always happy and seemed to enjoy life with a good and natural appetite. I felt very proud and satisfied to love him, but...

Suddenly John told me that he was in trouble, that his business had deceived him, and he had to leave his job and go back to the United States. Our good-bye was sad, filled with love, promises, and tears—my heart was aching, but life continued at its fast and intense pace. I was in residency training with at least ten days of night duty a month, nights which were always followed by a full day's work. I loved my work and gave my life to it.

All John left me at our good-bye meeting in Hamburg, besides a broken heart, was his red and black blanket, which I have kept to this today.

GYNECOLOGIC ENDOSCOPIC SURGERY AS PROMOTER OF MINIMALLY INVASIVE SURGERY (MIS) FOR ALL SURGICAL SPECIALTIES WORLDWIDE (1970–2011)

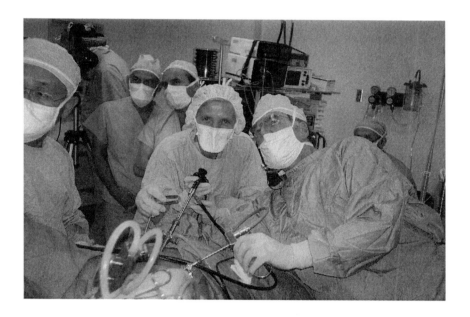

In 1970, Kurt Semm joined the Kiel University Department of Obstetrics and Gynecology as director. He was a Bavarian coming from Munich to Kiel, in Schleswig-Holstein, the northernmost German state. In American cultural geography, this amounts to a southerner from Tennessee entering the high society of Boston. With his distinctive Bavarian accent, he told us within the first few days that the days of open surgery with large incisions will soon be history; we would be changing to laparoscopic surgery with minimal access but better vision. For the readers' information, this means that when entering the abdomen, we went from a large twenty-centimeter incision to three small incisions measuring half a centimeter each. This surgical technique results in smaller scars, a faster healing period, and much less pain.

Kurt Semm had invented a CO_2 insufflation apparatus that electronically controlled the flow of CO_2 gas into the abdominal cavity. He used an endoscope to visualize the abdomen and ports, through which he inserted instruments to perform surgery and thus heal disease. The earlier use of air had already been abolished.

These were the early days, in 1970 and 1972, of laparoscopy as a surgical technique (in gynecology, we looked into the abdominal cavity and performed sterilizations and resected small tumors). Endoscopic surgery for general surgeons (e.g., for gallbladder surgery and bowel resections), orthopedic surgeons, cardiac surgeons (for bypass surgery) and for ear, nose, and throat surgeons and others came much later.

Laparoscopic/minimally invasive surgery, with its high success rates, is widely accepted today. New instrumentations are being continually developed and robotic surgery has made great advancements in the field. Laparoscopic surgery has replaced conventional surgery in up to 70 percent of all surgical procedures. However, in the early days, only the surgeon could see through the endoscope and thus a director telling us he can see well when the assistants saw nothing was questionable, or let us just say *challenging*. Every once in a while, Kurt Semm allowed us to have a look into the abdominal cavity, but it was difficult to judge the surgery. The technique was subject to much criticism even in our own hospital. The introduction of video laparoscopy, whereby everyone in the room could watch the surgery on the video screen, did not occur until ten years later. Kurt was a pioneer and a great instrument designer; they still call him the father of gynecological endoscopic surgery.

One day our new director asked, "Who wants to join my team to develop this surgical field?" There was silence in our group of thirty doctors; they all thought he was crazy. I raised my arm; I was the only female colleague and I was pregnant (in 1970 I had married and was pregnant with my first son). I said, "It's a fascinating approach, but I just wish we could have a better look at what you are doing."

"What am I to do with a woman?" Kurt Semm answered. This was typical of the male prejudice that every female surgeon still encounters in the western world. Interestingly, this is not the case in Asia, where female patients prefer female surgeons. However, I joined him and thus became a contemporary witness of innovative surgical developments, and, with time, a world-famous laparoscopic surgeon in my own right. But it was a rocky road. Why?

Georg Kelling performed the first endoscopic surgery, and viewed the stomach of a dog using Nitze's cystoscope and an air insufflation apparatus on the occasion of a meeting of natural scientists in Hamburg, Germany in 1901. The technique was not further developed until the 1940s: in France, by Raoul

Palmer, and in Germany by Hans Frangenheim. In 1967, Kurt Semm began to initiate developments in this surgical field, and I joined him from 1970 onward. We began to publish articles and hold lectures on laparoscopy around the world; however, the acceptance of Kurt Semm's technique was arduous and slow.

In 1972 I presented a paper on a series of patients who had been successfully operated on laparoscopically at a gynecological conference in Germany. After my presentation a very famous German professor, Professor Ober, approached me and said, "Young doctor, you have a good chance of making a successful career in gynecology, but please stop performing and talking about this ridiculous surgical procedure you call laparoscopy."

When I said, "But, Professor Ober, these patients were all successfully operated without cutting open the abdomen and were very satisfied," he just walked away. It took thirty years for gynecologists in Germany to really accept the technique. Kurt Semm and I were expelled from the German Society for Obstetrics and Gynecology and Kurt Semm had to undergo a brain scan to prove he had no brain damage.

In 1981, after we accomplished the first laparoscopic removal of an appendix in Kiel, the surgeons jumped on the bandwagon and began performing laparoscopic appendectomy. The first laparoscopic gallbladder resection followed in 1987, performed by Philippe Mouret. In 1986, the Kiel School introduced video laparoscopy, as did Camran Nezhat in the USA. From these years onward, laparoscopic surgery could be viewed on the video screen. Work on imaging steadily progressed from camera and light source development to the invention of the rod lens, from one-chip to three-chip cameras, and to high definition television.

By 1990, all medical disciplines were applying this fantastic, minimally invasive surgery that is not only medically effective, but also avoids larger incisions, prevents pain, shortens hospital stays, and reintegrates patients rapidly back into their family and professional life. Healthcare providers request it in different surgical fields, and it is certainly economic and cost-effective. Laparoscopic hysterectomy, bowel surgery, splenectomy, and other surgeries are now accepted endoscopic procedures and even requisitioned by many insurance companies.

During the years 1985–95, under the fabulous guidance of the American visionary, Jordan Phillips, Kurt Semm and I travelled eighty-seven times to the USA to hold endoscopic (laparoscopic) training courses. We performed surgeries and held lectures, always staying three days each on the East and West coasts, or in the Midwest, in order to teach this technique to American doctors. Jordan founded the American Association of Gynecologic Laparoscopists, which today is simply referred to as the AAGL, and is associated with the phrase "Advancing Minimally Invasive Gynecology Worldwide." There are eight thousand members worldwide.

The use of live surgery in the training of medical doctors has developed gradually. Direct transmission from the operation room (OR) enables a surgeon's skill to be observed by a large audience at another location, often thousands of miles away at a medical conference. These live surgical events have been integrated into medical conferences around the world in all disciplines. The patient is more secure as well, since the complete surgical procedure is documented by video. I have operated at numerous locations on all continents and was always received by my medical colleagues with the highest respect and friendship.

Apparatus and instrument development, in continuous cooperation with the medical technical industry, has led to new features for coagulation, stilling blood loss, laparoscopic suturing, and the introduction of robotics. Instruments went from two to multiple degrees of liberty, from straight to rotating, multifunctional, articulated, and robotic forms. Precision surgery by means of an enlarged visual image and small or even single port entries for an instrument set with multiple degrees of liberty has become a reality.

In the gynecological field, we also developed the visual exploration of the uterine cavity and the womb, called hysteroscopy. The first light guide dates back to Bozzini, over two centuries ago, and in Germany,

Hans Lindemann from Hamburg laid the groundwork for this technique. Hysteroscopy with a saline solution has become one of my favorite surgical techniques.

In Germany and Europe, as well as worldwide, many professional societies for endoscopic surgery have been founded. I have been president and general secretary of many of the societies for gynecologic laparoscopy and have published on laparoscopic and hysteroscopic surgeries in many high-ranking journals. In later years, I became honorary president and honorary member of many medical societies; people seemed to like my professional approach.

In November 2010, I was the honorary chair of the prestigious AAGL meeting in Las Vegas. This was a huge honor for a German, but of course the world picture has changed. America has opened to the world. We celebrated this occasion in Las Vegas together with my best student and successor in the Kiel School of Gynecological Endoscopy, University of Schleswig-Holstein, Germany, Thoralf Schollmeyer; the president of the AAGL 2010 annual meeting, C. Y. Liu, and his wife; and John.

The Vietnam and the Iraq wars, which were fought with great pride and a certain mission by the Americans, have also brought them many enemies. The opening of the USA to the world, on so many levels, has become more evident recently. A black president, Barack Obama, as much as he may be criticized within the country, is a phenomenal change, and his strategies are well-accepted around the world. Together with his government, he has reshaped the world's image of America.

When I started in gynecology in 1968, I was the only female among thirty male colleagues and had to prove myself over and over again in order to get ahead in a German university hospital, but with good academic work you always progress. I was also the first female professor in our specialty in Germany. Of course, I had to let several of my male colleagues pass me by, but it did not hurt me, and in the long run we all became good friends. On the contrary, if you have to fight for something, you enjoy the success even more. Today, 60 percent of the doctors in the Kiel Department of Obstetrics and Gynecology are female.

It may hurt at times, but it seems to me you always win in life if you give way to others.

MY MEDICAL LIFE AND FRIENDSHIP WITH KURT SEMM (1970–95)

Our First Meeting

Even though I have already mentioned several of these events earlier, I would like to share with you my experiences, both personally and medically, with my teacher, Kurt Semm.

Back from working in the Amazon Hospital Albert Schweitzer in Peru for a short three-month period in 1969–70, I had to finally decide which medical specialty I wished to pursue. General surgery was quite appealing to me, but it required strength and endurance for the long procedures. My friend and colleague Jim Dalrymple, a British general surgeon who worked for ten years in the Amazon hospital, was a great teacher and advised me to apply for a surgical specialization.

In 1969, I sent four applications from Peru for residency training to the Kiel University Departments of Ophthalmology, Pediatrics, General Surgery, and Gynecology. Within ten days I had an answer from Kurt Semm, the new director of the Department of Gynecology. He wrote that on my return I could immediately start work in his department. He didn't need any further papers from me, a "jungle girl" was always welcome. That is how I started in the field of gynecology, which includes not only gynecological surgical procedures but also endocrinology, oncology, obstetrics, and reproductive medicine. I gradually learned to live and love this specialization, which deals intensively with the beginning of life and accompanies a woman until the end of life's adventures.

After joining the Department of Gynecology and Obstetrics, I had to adjust to the strict rules of a German university hospital. I was thirty years old and eager to get a good academic and practical education; Kurt Semm was forty-three years old. In the jungle, as much as I liked my work there, I felt that I had to have more specific knowledge and skill in one area of medicine to be able to really help people.

Kurt was a stout Bavarian, and it was difficult for a Viennese "jungle girl" to admire. He was very direct, said everything he meant, and behaved quite differently to most of the colleagues working with us. He had been married for twelve years to Roswitha, a charming, slender, and good-looking lady who originated from former Prussia. She was a medical technologist who had worked together with Kurt in Munich, but she was no longer working in Kiel. Kurt and Roswitha had no children; I heard that there was a problem of infertility. Kurt Semm had founded the German Society of Reproductive Medicine in 1956, which meant that he definitely supported the wish of couples to have children.

Neither Kurt nor I fit into the strict pattern of a northern German university. He was the almighty director, and I was just a young female beginner in the field. Kurt had founded several German and international organizations and was well renowned.

When we first met, we skeptically analyzed each other. He was a tall and extremely good-looking man; his smile was open and he looked inquisitively into my eyes. He wanted to know everything about my life, and he spent a lot of time talking to me. I could feel that he liked me as a woman but did not hold a particularly high opinion of females in the profession. For him, male colleagues had the right to pursue scientific and clinical research; women belonged with the children and in the kitchen. For a long time, I was the only female assistant.

Kurt Semm had already achieved a lot in life. He had published many papers and had been appointed director of a university hospital at forty-three years old—that was really something. After telling him about my work in the jungle hospital with a lot of practical surgical experience and about my previous work in Kiel and in southern Germany, he smiled. I felt rather abashed and could not open myself to him easily, although I liked him. I had the feeling that it would be difficult for him to accept me as a professional, but that it would be easier for him to accept me personally.

These early years of working together were challenging in many ways. In the department, there quickly emerged two groups: the old gang with Professor Luh and the new group with Professor Semm. I definitely joined the new endoscopic surgery group with Professor Semm, which was then in its infancy.

I was Kurt Semm's private assistant. My job was to take care of our patients who were privately insured and who were treated by the director and the senior staff only. I learned quickly that despite all his achievements, Kurt Semm suffered from not having children and privately was not a particularly happy man.

I started well in this specialty; I loved my work, had many night duties, and started to do scientific experiments in my free time. After five months, one morning at a faculty meeting—all doctors met every morning at 7:30 for fifteen to twenty minutes in the Litzman Library—Kurt announced, "I am General Secretary of the International Society of Fertility and Sterility (IFFS) and am organizing the next World Congress in Tokyo in 1971. Who can give a presentation in Tokyo?" There was silence. So far, all of us had only presented papers at local German meetings in our specialty. After a while he said, "It has to be in English, of course." We all knew that Kurt Semm's English was quite poor, and he had a very Bavarian accent.

I raised my hand rather reluctantly and said that I had just finished an experiment on the interaction of sperm antibodies on fertilization, which I had sent off to be published in the journal *Fertility and Sterility*.

He looked at me and said, "Isn't there a male colleague who can present a paper?"

Again, there was a long silence until my dear friend Willi Phillipp said, "I have something on tubal anatomy, but Lisa will have to translate it and present it for me, as my English is poor."

Kurt Semm looked at me and said, "Well, then she can also translate mine into English." This initiated my career with Kurt as translator and traveling partner to help with his lectures. We sent off three papers to be presented and only mine was accepted. Kurt had a "state of the art" paper in gynecological endoscopic surgery, but he was totally astonished that my paper was the only free paper accepted.

Kurt, Roswitha, and I all traveled to Tokyo. This was my first big international conference and I really enjoyed it. I did not spend much time with Roswitha and Kurt, but on one occasion I told them that I would like to invite them to my wedding with Reza.

Some months later, when I was pregnant, I consulted Kurt as my obstetrician. He treated me correctly but made remarked that I could have waited to become pregnant until I had finished my residency. A pregnant colleague was a thorn in his eye. He delivered all of my three children but could never understand why, with all my positive medical achievements, I wanted to have children.

Just to finalize our personal friendship and love, it was I who diagnosed Roswitha's breast cancer. I accompanied Roswitha throughout her illness until she died in 1986. We had very close family and neighborly relations in Kiel.

Eight years later, in 1994, Kurt married my dear friend, Isolde, a vibrant and lovely Irish girl. This was already the year of his official retirement. He now had a new family with their wonderful children, Tara and Kurt-Patrick.

Isolde had joined the department as a young Irish-American woman. One day, while Isolde was assisting me, Kurt stormed into the operating theater because someone had reported to him that I was using bipolar coagulation, which he had forbidden. Kurt screamed, "You will destroy my reputation with such bad surgery." We were startled and Isolde said, "How can you dare to speak like that to Professor Mettler, you male chauvinist!" He had a rough outside but a soft heart.

Our two families had very close ties during Kurt and Isolde's last years in Kiel. Out of friendship and admiration for Kurt, my family decided to buy his house and his yacht, a forty-three-foot Finish Nauticat, named Okeanos, which we still sail today on the Baltic.

Kurt and his family moved to Tucson, Arizona in 1996 and visited us every year for several weeks in Kiel. I was also their regular guest in Tucson. Professionally, Kurt never thought that I could keep his endoscopic surgery going, although in the first years after his retirement we performed more endoscopic surgeries in Kiel than ever before. Women's power was something he never could and never wanted to accept.

MY ACTIVITIES WITH KURT SEMM AND THE PROPAGATION OF GYNECOLOGICAL ENDOSCOPIC SURGERY WORLDWIDE (1970–95)

In Kiel we had good success with our early experiences in endoscopic (minimally invasive) gynecologic surgery, and Kurt Semm can rightly be considered the father of laparoscopic surgery worldwide. As Kurt was a technical engineer as well as a medical doctor with a strong Catholic-Jesuit education, everything had to be exactly 100 percent correct.

New instruments were developed daily and sent to his brother Horst in Munich for refinement. Kurt's brother was a mechanical engineer, and he and Kurt had established their own surgical instrument and apparatus company, called WISAP, in Munich. The instruments were always promptly delivered to Kiel and we could try them out within a few days. These instruments gave us much better working conditions than many of the other instruments available at that time.

In 1972, I presented a paper on ovarian cyst resection at the annual meeting of the German Society of Obstetrics and Gynecology in Freiburg. After this lecture, the famous and well-renowned Professor Ober said to me, "Young doctor, that was a nice presentation, but it's all nonsense. If you want to make headway in this specialty, stay away from Kurt Semm."

"But professor," I responded, "We do these surgeries daily."

"That's criminal," he told me. "You need to open the abdomen widely to heal patients, not through these small incisions and by looking through a laparoscope. That's not the way you perform correct surgery."

Well, I thought, *maybe he's right*. At that time, only the surgeon could see the inside the patient through the scope. As an assistant doctor, I was occasionally allowed a glance through the laparoscope, but I usually had to assist by pure intuition. Only the professor could see inside the patient. I could not really judge if he was doing a good job. Later, teaching scopes with a second light channel were developed and allowed the assistant to see the surgery as well.

After 1980, video laparoscopy was introduced and propagated mostly through the intensive work of my friend Camran Nezhat, in Atlanta and San Francisco. Camran also had to fight for recognition of the brilliant laparoscopic surgery he performed in the USA in the early 1980s.

Kurt often screamed at me during surgery when I was holding the camera. It was difficult to direct the camera at the area where he wanted to work, as I couldn't see it. When I told him about Professor Ober's remark, he got furious and wanted to sue him; however, I saw that most of our patients were recovering very well after the surgery, and I thoroughly enjoyed working with my teacher.

There was plenty of opposition to the endoscopic team within our own hospital, as well as in the city of Kiel, in Germany, and worldwide. We sometimes felt like criminals, but Kurt's conviction that "one day, they will understand" persuaded me and other colleagues to carry on. Of course, as in any other surgical procedures, there were times when we had to do a second procedure, or patients continued to have pain. Two patients founded the Society of Laparoscopically Damaged Patients and invited us for discussions. Kurt said to me, "That's something you can deal with. I don't want to waste my time." These discussions with patients were mostly too fantastic to describe.

Not only did the German Society of Obstetrics and Gynecology threaten to expel us, but Kurt Semm also had to undergo a brain scan and MRI to prove that his mind was healthy. An article had appeared in the German magazine *Spiegel* reporting that a mentally disturbed man was the director of the Kiel University Department of Obstetrics and Gynecology and was performing crazy surgeries. It was suspected that Kurt had some abnormal areas in his brain; however, no brain alterations or scars were detected.

All our leading colleagues in the medical faculty in Kiel supported Kurt because the complication rate was not higher than after open surgery; on the contrary, it was much lower, and the patients were very happy.

The rumor of laparoscopic surgery spread. In these early years, as I was a female, I was only allowed to assist, but quite a few of our male colleagues also performed an increasing amount of surgeries laparoscopically.

One day in 1973, Professor Jan Behrman, the director of the Ann Arbor Gynecology Department and president of the American Society of Obstetrics and Gynecology, arrived in Kiel without notice. The receptionist in the hospital called the operating theater where Kurt was performing an adnexectomy on a seventy-eight-year-old patient with benign ovarian cysts. I was pregnant at the time and responsible, together with another colleague, for the anesthesia procedure. Prior to the set-up of the Department of Anesthesia in 1975, we performed our own anesthesia procedures. Kurt told me to go and see who the American visitor was. I welcomed Jan Behrman who said, "I've come over to Germany to go hunting, but I also want to see if that criminal Kurt Semm really does perform other laparoscopic surgical procedures besides sterilizations and diagnostic laparoscopies, which we are all doing." I explained that Professor Semm was just now performing an adnexectomy. Dr. Behrman asked whether he could observe, and I replied, "Why not?" and took him to the operating theater.

Kurt explained the whole case to him and let him use the teaching scope. They took pictures with our old Leica and our guest seemed to be satisfied. After the surgery, he thanked us, and Kurt, who knew Jan Behrman from international conferences, wanted to invite him for a chat, but Jan told him, "I have to leave for my hunting trip, but it was certainly worthwhile coming to Kiel. I am now a firm supporter of yours," which he really was in the years that followed.

Kurt was meticulously precise and prepared everything before he performed surgical endoscopic procedures outside of Kiel. On one trip to Mumbai (or Bombay, as it was called then) in the mid-seventies, he had written numerous letters to his friend, Professor Narges Motashaw, in preparation for a case of ovarian and infertility surgery. I was supposed to assist Kurt and while inspecting Dr. Motashaw's preparations—the patient was already sleeping—Kurt noticed that Dr. Motashaw wanted him to enter the abdominal cavity with a ten-millimeter trocar. He had written to her previously that he entered the abdomen with a five-millimeter trocar and then dilated to a ten-millimeter trocar. There was, however, no five-millimeter trocar. Kurt looked at me and said, "We are leaving; we're not doing this surgery." There was an icy atmosphere in the operating theater, which held at least thirty visiting doctors and the patient, who was already under anesthesia.

As the grand seignior left, everybody turned to me. I had never performed an abdominal laparoscopic entry and had only watched five-millimeter entries that were then dilated to ten-millimeter entries for the optic trocar. "Dr. Lisa," people said. "Go ahead." I was startled and did not know what to answer. All eyes were on me, and I saw no way of leaving the operating theater. With all my inner prayers and all my courage, I went ahead and performed the surgery. It was, in fact, my first laparoscopic abdominal entry. Many things could have gone wrong, but nothing adverse happened; the case was successful.

Back in Kiel, Kurt Semm did not speak to me for several weeks. He just said, "You could have put an end to all my laparoscopic surgery if you had had problems in Mumbai." Well, that is how he was!

We developed many new laparoscopic strategies and when I said we have to publish these, he answered, "That is not necessary; people believe me." But the problem was that people did not believe him. When we published our first statistical papers in the 1980s, he said, "Don't even mention complications. You have complications; I have none." He had the golden fingers of a laparoscopic surgeon and we didn't. Sometimes it was not easy to work with him, but we loved him and were carried along by his enthusiasm for laparoscopic surgery.

In 1981 we performed the first endoscopic appendectomy in the world, and many followed. Many general surgeons considered this approach criminal. Professor Schreiber, president of the German Society of General Surgery, publically condemned our laparoscopic approach. He later regretted it and apologized publicly. He told Kurt, in front of other people, "I am ashamed. I have made a great mistake in misjudging this surgical approach via the laparoscope. Please accept my apologies."

After the first twenty endoscopic appendectomies, we prepared a manuscript with splendid pictures of this new, minimally invasive surgical approach to appendectomy for the prestigious journal *Archives of Gynecology*. This new term, "minimally invasive," described our surgical approach better than laparoscopic surgery. Although we had included all the classical surgical steps performed via laparotomy (open surgery), we received the manuscript back with the remark, "Accepting such nonsense is not appropriate for this distinguished publishing house. Appendectomy has to be performed by laparotomy with open access to the abdomen."

It took another year until endoscopic appendectomy was finally accepted at the 1982 pan-American conference in Costa Rica and even honored with the annual prize of that society. It was published in *Advances in Pelviscopic Surgery* and was extremely well received.

Laparoscopic assisted vaginal hysterectomy had been performed in our department since 1984, but it was considered poor vaginal surgery, as those surgeons experienced in vaginal surgery said that they did not need the laparoscopic view to help them. We performed laparoscopic assisted vaginal surgeries but were afraid to publish our results, as the German Society of Obstetrics and Gynecology still condemned this approach.

Between 1986 and 1995, the Kiel team of laparoscopic and hysteroscopic surgeons made more than eighty trips to the USA to teach these techniques. Dr. Jordan Philipps, the wonderful organizer and founder of the American Association of Gynecological Laparoscopy (AAGL) always scheduled one two-day meeting on the East Coast and one on the West Coast, or one up North and one down South. Our visits were well-advertised to our American colleagues. We spent some great weeks traveling all over the USA. Back home, we had to work double-time to make up for our absence from the hospital. Our enthusiasm was driven by Kurt's continuous efforts to propagate this surgery.

We always received the money for the plane tickets in cash. One day in Houston, before leaving the hospital, Kurt handed me a brown paper bag with the money and told me to take good care of it. We were in a hurry and quickly grabbed a hamburger at a kiosk outside the hospital and then took the taxi to the airport. Just before boarding, Kurt said, "Lisa, you've got the money. Let's give it to Hans Riedel, Peter Stoll, and everyone now." Wow, at that moment I remembered that I had put the brown paper bag next to the wastepaper basket while I was eating my hamburger and had forgotten to pick it up again. Everyone screamed at me when I told them. I took a taxi back to the hospital, found the brown paper bag still standing beside the wastepaper basket, smiling at me, and, can you believe it, I even made it back to the plane on time. The icy reception Kurt gave me when he received the bag initiated several days of silence between us.

Somehow we had to learn that, in contrast to European medical meetings, in the USA, our American colleagues were waiting for lectures and ready for practical training at seven o'clock in the morning. When we all said good night, usually late in the evening, Kurt would say to me, "You take the early lectures when people are still half-asleep and I'll wake them up after nine o'clock."

There was a huge amount of interest in our endoscopic procedures among our medical colleagues. In Kiel we continued to have guests from all around the world and, of course, from Germany. In 1990, I founded the Kiel School of Gynecological Endoscopy to give structure to our teaching.

Kurt first found the idea totally unnecessary, but finally accepted the establishment of the school.

It wasn't until 1991 that Kurt introduced the Classic Intrafascial Subtotal Hysterectomy (CISH). This was due to a number of reasons. I describe the following incident lightly, but it was in effect the resurrection hour of subtotal hysterectomy, which carries many advantages for women.

We were holding a laparoscopy teaching course at the Riverside Hospital in Baltimore, Maryland, with Jim Dorsey when suddenly most of the visitors disappeared from our operating theater (OT), where Kurt was performing a laparoscopic myomectomy, and went to watch another teacher, Harry Reich, perform a total laparoscopic hysterectomy in the adjacent OT. These were the days before transmission by satellite or other media, and Kurt sent me over to the other OT to see what was going on. I reported that Harry had performed what he dared to call a laparoscopic assisted vaginal hysterectomy. In Germany, we would never have dared to use this term, as most German gynecologists were very much against laparoscopic surgery. We just called it laparoscopic assistance to vaginal hysterectomy.

On our flight back to Germany, Kurt designed a "superior alternative," the laparoscopic subtotal hysterectomy (LSH), to Harry's LAVH, which seemed to have attracted so much attention. Kurt performed the procedure for the first time the following Saturday in Kiel. He preferred to operate with just a select team of doctors. The outcome was successful and the department primarily performed this type of hysterectomy in the coming years. We worked hard for the comeback of the subtotal hysterectomy as an endoscopic procedure. This surgical procedure changed world perspectives in our field.

In the years 1986–95 we travelled throughout Europe and the world holding lectures on gynecological endoscopic surgery. Many medical colleagues asked us to perform endoscopic surgical procedures on their patients so that they could learn the new techniques. Whenever we reached a new city and hotel, Kurt always told the receptionist, "I am Professor Kurt Semm. I have developed this new technique and of course I am to have the best room. Somehow, many times, I ended up with the best view or the larger room, and he was always jealous. We had our funny little arguments and often ended up changing rooms.

Back in Kiel, I particularly enjoyed doing telesurgical procedures as this was easier and allowed us to spend more time at home with our families. In the OT there was always a lot of anxiety and action whenever we transmitted live surgery to San Francisco, London, New York, or any other place in the world.

In Kiel we continued to perform extensive laparoscopic surgery and developed modern reproductive medical techniques. We had many famous patients. One day Kurt announced at the morning staff meeting, "Today, someone has to collect Niki Lauda from the airport in Hamburg. We'll do his semen analysis and tomorrow I'll perform a laparoscopy on his wife. They want to have children." One of Kurt's eager followers, Hans Riedel, volunteered to collect Niki Lauder with his

Mercedes. Niki Lauda was a famous Formula One racing driver from Austria who today owns his own airlines: Niki and Lauda Airlines.

When the time came to collect Niki, Hans was busy in the operating theater, and I was sent on my way. I was excited to meet this racing star and my knees were shaking. Niki was an impressive man. I was very nervous but tried to appear cool. I liked his wife and drove them back to Kiel in my Porsche with a bubbling heart. We had an interesting conversation and the semen analysis was quickly explained. What a pleasure to drive a Formula One champion!

In the evening, Kurt was ready to drive Niki back to Hamburg. Kiel is about one hundred kilometers north of Hamburg, but Niki said, "I prefer to drive with my friend Lisa, as she has a racing car." Maybe one day, we'll get some free flights, as after their visit with us they had two children. Another secret patient was the beautiful Italian actress Sophia Loren, but here the doctor remains quiet.

Kurt Semm was general secretary and president of numerous professional societies and received various honors from many countries, governments, and institutions. He was very proud to receive the Bavarian and the German Cross of Honor (Bundesverdienstkreuz am Bande). He became a member of the famous Leopoldina (the German Society of Elected Scientists), and was awarded honorary membership not only of the German but also of the International Federation of Obstetrics and Gynecology (FIGO), and of Reproductive Medicine and of Gynecological Endoscopy. He was also awarded an honorary membership of the American Society of General Surgery.

Kurt died in Tucson, Arizona in 2003. In accordance with his wishes, he was brought back to Germany and buried in his family tomb in the München-Solln cemetery. More than twenty colleagues and coworkers from Kiel attended his funeral service in Munich in 2003 where his family, friends, and a huge medical following gave him his well-merited last honors. His eight-year-old son Kurt-Patrick carried the honor pins and ribbons on a blue pillow.

It was good-bye to a man who had opened a new field of surgery for the whole world: for patients, for the health care systems, for the medical technology industry, and for generations of doctors to come. Kurt Semm is the father of surgical endoscopy in Germany and worldwide.

FAMILY LIFE WITH REZA AND OUR CHILDREN BIJAN-SEBASTIAN, ALEXANDER-FIRUS, AND MORITZ-STEFAN

In 1970 I married my medical colleague and friend Reza, who came from Tehran, Iran, and who had studied medicine with me in Tübingen and Kiel. We were in a group of four students who took all our major exams together. Only during my semesters in Vienna was Reza in Tübingen. The decision to marry met with opposition from both our families due to the differences in family background and religion and required us to place a lot of trust in each other. For a long time we had considered ourselves no more than friends, but that changed. Reza chose to specialize in pathology and I in obstetrics and gynecology.

We have three wonderful sons—two of them are lawyers and one a medical student—and three grandchildren: Natalia, Heriberto, and Valentina. Our life centered on the family and the university in Kiel. Occasionally, we took study leaves in other countries and kept up a close relationship with our Iranian family. As university professors, we were both actively engaged in research, teaching, and clinical practice. Reza became an internationally renowned scientist in the field of hematopathology. Two boys now live in Miami, Florida, and one lives in Frankfurt, Germany.

Besides our own children, we also brought up five nephews and one niece: Majid, Hamid, Hamed, Maryam, Kia, and Mani who, due to the political situation in Iran (revolution of 1970, which ended the rule of the Shah and introduced the religious regime under Ayatollah Khomeini), were sent to Germany for their schooling at a very young age. With seven boys in the house, there was always action. The thirty-five years of our marriage passed in perfect harmony, and in loving, raising, and educating the children. Along with all my professional activities, life progressed like a beautiful, mighty river that never stops. I had not heard a word from John in all those years.

In 2005 Reza died, totally unexpectedly, of a heart attack. The continuous flow of the river suddenly took an abrupt turn and halted. I will never forget this life, which continues through my three boys and nephews.

IN VITRO FERTILIZATION AND EMBRYO TRANSFER (IVF–ET): THE TEST TUBE TECHNIQUE

There have been numerous amazing discoveries in the fields of medicine, genetics, and physiology in the twentieth century, a few of which include: imaging techniques that allow visual access of different layers and organs of the body, the human genome, and early cancer detection. However, no cancer cure is available as yet.

In my estimation, the greatest medical achievement of the twentieth century was the birth of the first test tube baby, Louise Brown, in 1978. This was made possible by the technique of in vitro fertilization and embryo transfer, first performed by Robert Edwards and Patrick Steptoe. Before this, nobody could have imagined that extracorporeal conception (the creation of a baby through the unification of egg and sperm outside the human womb), was possible. On the contrary, three centuries ago it was still thought that the female was created in the sperm and it was Van Beer (1792–1876) who first described the mammalian egg.

Thirty-two years after the birth of Louise Brown, in 2010, the Nobel Prize in medicine and physiology was finally awarded to Robert Edwards from Cambridge, Great Britain. This is a major achievement for Bob Edwards and for all of us who apply this technique in clinical medicine.

In 1976, I did a few months of elective research in the physiological laboratory of Bob Edwards in Cambridge. In my research laboratory in Kiel, in an attempt to develop an alternative contraceptive method, we used an experimental in vitro fertilization model to test antibodies of eggs and sperm in their capacity to impede fertilization. I had met Bob Edwards at a number of medical meetings and was a supporter of the IVF technique. At that time, our British colleagues had achieved one ectopic human pregnancy and were seriously engaged in the project. Bob Edwards, a brilliant scientist and wonderful teacher, gave me so much encouragement and support that we in Kiel were among the first to successfully treat patients who wanted to have children with this technique. The birth of the first successful test tube baby encouraged a superb group of scientists to get together internationally to work in this field.

After their success, the British colleagues were not very communicative; however, there was the Melbourne group around Alan Trounson and Carl Wood, who had also reported their first successful cases. They were willing to discuss the techniques with everyone. I decided to travel to Australia after we had done fifty embryo transfers without a successful pregnancy. Can you believe that the thirty days I was in Melbourne, we were only in the lab and the hospital, and made no outside visits?

Our first successful pregnancy did not occur until after Bob Edwards's visit to Kiel, when he told me, "Lisa, there shouldn't be a door between the laboratory and the egg retrieval room. Remove the door." We removed the door and were successful. Why did he, as a biologist, say that?

The biologist-embryologist does 50 percent of the work, and the clinician does the other 50 percent. Therefore, the embryologist must be present at the moment of egg retrieval and not shut off by a wall.

I got to know Melbourne much later. This year, in December 2011, as General Secretary of the International Academy of Human Reproduction, I am invited back to Melbourne for our World Congress. In 1981, we held the first World Congress of Human Reproduction in Kiel.

After our first successful pregnancies, we had many patients and openly discussed the technique with the media. There was opposition from many ethical groups who accused us of human selection and misunderstood our goal of helping childless couples. However, I have to admit that once this technology proved to be successful, it did of course open the door for the abuse of the technique.

In the beginning, we had to establish our own ethical laws for IVF treatment in patients, as nobody else was interested. After 1990, government agencies around the world and professional groups drafted laws and restrictions for this treatment. Laboratory and clinical research resulted in further advances, such as the intracytoplasmatic sperm injection (ICSI) in 1993 used to treat sperm-related infertility problems. A single sperm is injected into a mature egg, and the fertilized egg is then placed in a woman's uterus or fallopian tube.

Many countries have excellent prospective data of all treatment cycles performed per year. The German DIR registry collects all treatment cycles performed annually and evaluates the data of all 110 centers and compares each center's data to the data of the other centers.

More than five million IVF/ET babies have been born around the world. In the early 1980s, acceptance of the technology was very difficult, as society was reluctant to believe in its merits. I personally received a number of anonymous phone calls with death threats. We had police protection around our home in Kiel and, luckily, they detected a bomb was beneath my car before it had a chance to detonate. One night there was a break-in at our laboratory and some experimental work was destroyed. Later a feminist group named Rote Zora (Red Zora), confessed to the break-in, as they believed we forced women to get pregnant against their will. We had to give detailed explanations to avoid misunderstandings. The happiness of our patients, of women who were able to give birth, prevailed over these transient problems.

Today, reproductive medicine has a firm standing, and we have to meet head-on all positive and negative developments in this field. Let me just say that according to our current understanding, human cloning must not be allowed, as it still leads to disastrous outcomes. Preimplantation genetic screening (PGD) is forbidden in Germany by law. However, PGD can recognize genetic abnormalities in the early embryonic stage, in the eight–cell stage (two days after conception), and up to the blastocyst stage (four days after conception). Only unaffected embryos are then implanted, thereby eliminating the dilemma of pregnancy termination following unfavorable prenatal diagnosis.

In 1981, when we organized the first World Congress of IVF in Kiel, we had only one hundred participants. Today, our World Congress of IVF and the European Congress of Human Reproduction (ESHRE) each attract between six and eight thousand participants.Δ122

LIFE AND WORK IN THE AMAZON HOSPITAL ALBERT SCHWEITZER IN THE PERUVIAN JUNGLE, 1966–67

In 1966 I joined the medical team of the Amazon hospital in Yarina Cocha in the flat jungle of Peru, about a thousand miles east of Lima. Having just completed two years of an internship with rotations in general surgery, internal medicine, and gynecology and obstetrics, I felt as if I was at the top of my profession, knew everything, and was now ready for my long-awaited dream to serve as a doctor in a missionary hospital. As a convinced Christian, I could think of nothing better than to work as a doctor and at the same time as a missionary, but I couldn't find a missionary hospital in the area I was interested in. As I had already traveled a bit, knew the basics of Spanish, and loved Latin America, my choice fell on this hospital with a monthly salary of U.S. $150. At that time, money had no value for me, and I arrived full of enthusiasm in Pucallpa.

I took the road over the Andes by car a year later, during one of my Lima visits, and we needed four days on a truck over very bad roads, partially destroyed by heavy rains. From Pucallpa, we drove on a small truck for three to four hours and then transferred to a large canoe, called a pequi-pequi, with a forty-horsepower motor for our trip down the river Ucayali. This was a luxurious, fast-running boat, as we passed many boats with only four horsepower motors.

Further north of Pucallpa, the Ucayali forms the main headwater of the Amazon River. After six or seven hours on this boat, we reached the entry of the large lagoon called Yarina Cocha, which extended over twenty kilometers into the jungle, and the Amazon Hospital Albert Schweitzer. The San Francisco river originally formed the lagoon. Boats could only reach Yarina, the biggest village along the lake, in the high water season. In the low water season, only water planes could reach the hospital. I learned quickly that rivers are the streets of the jungle. Today, Yarina can be reached by land over a bumpy road, but this has only developed over the last twenty years.

The Amazon Hospital Albert Schweitzer was situated on a lovely slope alongside the lagoon, where an area of about two hundred hectares had been cut out of the jungle. I saw stone and wooden houses as well as a huge Indian campamiento. In the campamiento, the families of the patients we hospitalized could live and support their loved ones. Our patients came from the indigenous Indian tribes of the area, the Shipibo, Aguaruna, and Campa.

I spent the most wonderful and rewarding eighteen months working in this hospital, which greatly influenced my future life. The language in the hospital, the documentation, and everything else was Spanish; we talked to the patients in their native languages and in Spanish. I saw patients from six in the morning until two in the afternoon. For the most part, I spent the two-hour resting period in the afternoon waterskiing with my friend Raul, a Peruvian technical assistant, who was responsible for our boats. We then continued to work until eight in the evening. There was little free time, but spending time with the international staff after work was rewarding.

The hospital was founded by Theodor Binder in 1960 and internationally funded until 1980, when it became a national hospital. It is still up and running today. Albert Schweitzer, a German philosopher and medical doctor, had founded a successful hospital in Lambarene, a city in Gabon, Africa. Theodor Binder, an admirer of Albert Schweitzer, gained Schweitzer's permission to name his Amazonian hospital after him. Evidently, Albert Schweitzer once personally visited our hospital in Peru.

At first I received patients and assigned them to treatment groups. Many times I assisted our general surgeon and administered anesthesia. The surgical spectrum included all imaginable procedures, and I learned a lot. I very soon recognized how limited my medical experience really was and that I needed further training. We did not deliver babies in the hospital; we only received pathological cases. Many times I was rushed by motorbike or plane to distant places for obstetrical crisis situations.

Let me just mention some of my experiences. For four months I worked together with a British nurse, Jene, in a village of the Campa Indians. They allowed us females to see and examine their patients, but no male was allowed to approach the village. Quickly people heard about doctor Lilo and Jene. Females, as well as males, approached us with minor and major problems. We slept in hammocks and lived quite simply with these people from daybreak until sunset; then we listened to the mysterious noises of nature as we contemplated life or attempted to sleep. It took me many days to really sleep in a hammock. At that time, it did not seem romantic to me at all. We were, however, in telephone contact with the hospital and we could fly patients in and out and get appropriate medications. Some rare times we were invited to a campfire party to share meat with the Indians.

During the two months I spent working in the hospital's leper ward, I experienced the sad reality of the disease as I saw people losing their limbs and even dying. There was nothing we were able to do; luckily, no contamination occurred. Many of these patients preferred to live in the adjacent Shipibo campamiento—far from the major village, in the leper section. They did not want to be seen by their families anymore, as they looked ugly. They also needed comfort, conversation, and daily dressing of their wounds. I do remember a Shipibo-Peruvian mestizo school teacher telling me of her wonderful life and years with children in the Pachitea area, farther up the Ucayali river, where many Germans and British adventurers had tried to breed cattle. Many of these adventurers brought their families with them and she had taught some of these "blondy kids" and the local children, all with long, dark hair, to read and to write together. She had been educated in Lima with an educational program whose goal was to promote literacy among people living in the *selva* (the jungle) areas of Peru under President Bellaunde. She had worked in Terapoto, Pucallpa, and Iquitos, the larger cities of the Selva Peruana, but she really preferred to live in smaller villages with mostly Indians of different tribes. She had a husband who could not read or write, but he was a good hunter and the chief of his village. She had lived with him for twenty-three years; they were not officially married, but they respected and loved each other. They had three children, who were grown up. When her leprosy became very aggressive, she left the family without ever telling them where she went and came to the hospital. She helped me a lot, but we never embraced or had any close contact. Her Spanish was perfect. Once I asked her, "Don't you want to know what your children are doing?"

She replied, "No, they are good people and will find their ways. I was just their temporary guide in life, and now they have to face life themselves. You create and help your children grow, but then you have to let them go." What a wonderful philosophy; I asked myself how many children I would have and wondered how life would continue. Somehow, at that time, I never thought about the possibility of contracting leprosy, and we did our work very carefully, but it was still dangerous, and the risk of contamination was always there.

I was quickly taught the administration of anesthesia and given the full responsibility of doing so. Our general surgeon was a Swiss lady, Dr. Irene, and later it was Jim Dalryple, the famous Dr. Jim, an excellent British general surgeon. One long weekend, Irene flew to Lima, and then, of all times, I developed an acute appendicitis and needed surgery. Sergio, a young doctor like myself, was the only available surgeon. The two of us studied my case with the help of a medical book, more like a surgical atlas, and designed the individual steps he needed to take to find my appendix. I had severe pain at McBurney's point in my abdomen (which defines acute appendicitis), high leukocytes, and was vomiting. Sergio performed his first appendectomy on me. As I was in pain, there was no alternative. Luckily he had, like me, learned to give spinal anesthesia and, after the typical abdominal incision, he was able to discuss his surgical steps with me. Quickly he found the appendix, tied the appendicular artery, and skeletonized my appendix, which was swollen and infected, but not yet perforated. He said I was smiling the whole time and that inspired him to act properly. He was really sweet and we took a long time, so the nurse had to give me additional anesthesia. I survived and that speaks to Sergio's skill. He later became a dermatologist, and when we met, he often mentioned this surgery, which had played such a decisive role in both our destinies. He had decided not to become a surgeon, and I had convinced myself to become a gynecological surgeon.

Further up the lagoon, there was the camp of the Lingüístico de Verano, an American missionary group of Christian idealists who came for two to three years to live with their families in the jungle. They had built a village in the jungle, taught Spanish to the natives, and learned the native languages of the Shipibos, Aguarunas, and Campas with the aim of translating the Bible into these languages. They also planned to write down and alphabetize these languages. These American missionaries were extremely nice people who had given up their work back home in order to come to the jungle. They lived in comfortable houses and had airplanes at their disposal.

Our hospital had an agreement with them whereby they would fly us to patients. I liked the people, especially the pilots, who flew us to our destinations, but I could not agree with their mission. The reality of working with my patients showed me quickly that I could serve them very well as a medical doctor, and did not have to convince them of Christianity. The Christian religion, which is such a personal religion, was extremely difficult for them to understand, and I did not think it necessary to impose it upon them. However, the missionaries' endeavor to write down the Indian languages was an admirable one.

I remember it vividly—it was Thursday morning at six o'clock, and I could feel the drizzling rain coming down through the trees. I had a strange feeling in the pit of my stomach, which I had never felt before. I knew it wasn't physical. We all came together in the cafeteria area of the hospital around seven in the morning for our small breakfast, comprised of bread, fruit, and coffee. My dear friends and I made small talk. Later that morning we were notified suddenly that a Campa family desperately needed our help in delivering a half-born child in breech position. We notified one of our wonderful pilots and friend, Jim. He immediately started preparations with our small jungle plane, which was a four-seater. My friend Juliane and I grabbed our medical supplies and equipment and walked quickly toward the plane. With each step, there was a stronger and stronger feeling welling up inside of me, telling me not to go. I thought, how crazy! This is what I have worked for and lived for all these years. I suppressed this awful fear as well as I could. We boarded the plane, strapped ourselves in, and Jim started down the runway. The rain was coming down harder, and the little plane slid a bit on the unpaved runway. Soon we were airborne, but this feeling of fear was still strong inside me.

"Let's have a great rainy trip," Jim called back to us.

We tried to smile. "Keep your eyes on the road," I said to Jim. He laughed. After about an hour into our trip, the plane's motor started sputtering. Jim called back to us to hold on and told us he would try to find a safe place to land. Suddenly, just ahead of us, as the clouds broke temporarily, we could see that we were only a few hundred feet from a tropical hill in the slowly ascending rain forest.

"I'm going to climb above it!" Jim yelled. "Hold on!" The hill got closer and closer, and I knew we could not make it.

The last thing I remember was grabbing hold of Juliane and shouting, "I love you!" In a split-second, I heard a crash, and then everything went black. By some miracle, perhaps many hours later, I opened my eyes and found myself lodged in the high branches of three trees that had grown together. I looked down about forty feet and could see a small river below me. I tried to move, and, to my amazement, nothing seemed to be broken, although I was unbelievably sore. Slowly, I slid and climbed down the tree until my feet touched the blessed earth. No one will ever convince me that there is not a higher power! I knelt down for a moment on the wet ground and thanked God for saving my life! I knew then I would try with all my heart to return the gift to as many people as I could, and for as long as I could. My thoughts suddenly returned to my dear friends, Juliane and Jim. I called out desperately for them, but there was no answer. I searched the area for about an hour, but there were no signs of life or of the jungle plane. I quickly became aware that the best and only friend I had now, besides God, was the small river! I knew that if I followed the river north it would take me in the direction of our camp and hospital. I had a compass and quickly got my direction. The adrenalin was pumping, and I knew darkness was just two or three hours away. I started my trek in and along the small river feeling a mixture of unbelievable gratitude along with a certain fear of the unknown. How many miles would I have to walk? Would the animals be dangerous, especially at night when I could not see them? I remember walking many hours into the dark night, trying to convince myself that the strange animal sounds were actually my friends. I finally could walk no further and lay down under a tree. My eyes immediately fell closed, and I slept like I was dead. I was awakened by sunlight coming in jaggedly through the trees. There were ants crawling on my hand. I had no water or food, but I was not hungry, only thirsty. I knew I had to keep walking. The blessed river, my new and dear friend, suddenly ended in a dry bed. I followed this bed anyway and, after hours, reached another water arm of the jungle.

It took me two days, following small jungle rivers, to reach a site of Campa Indians who saved me. What can I say, it was a nightmare, but God wanted me to live, and here I am. Search planes later found the remnants of our plane and my friends, who had died. After the incident, I went to Lima to stay with Hannes and Inez, my dear friends, who asked no questions. They just let me live and decide what to do.

After two weeks I went back to the hospital and worked for some time as a river doctor. With the Amazon hospital's canoe, we approached numerous small villages of mestizos and American Indians along the Rio Pisqui, from the flat jungle up to the higher area where the beautiful Andes mountain range begins. We treated children and adults with medication, offered advice, and transported patients to the hospital when necessary. Many times we just explained how to boil the river water before drinking it. I became a specialist in the treatment of worms, a rampant disease among the natives.

Working on the rivers meant we learned to appreciate God's light of day and use it to the full extent. We had, of course, fires in the evening and occasionally used our petroleum lamps, but there was no electricity. We had ample time at night in the amacas on board to think about life and life's beauties. I became good friends with many Shipibos and have been back several times in later years to visit these small settlements. All my work showed me how limited my medical knowledge really was and how necessary it was to know one subject in our medical field more thoroughly. I wanted to learn more, to become a better doctor. Nevertheless, it was quite sad to leave all the good friends I had made over my months in the Amazon.

Today, Pucallpa and Yarina are connected by large settlements of American Indians and Peruvians who have moved to the jungle. Within an hour, you can reach Yarina from Pucallpa on a carretera, a paved road. In 1966, Pucallpa had only twenty-five thousand inhabitants and no paved streets; the city was quite muddy and slippery on rainy days. However, the tropical climate made up for any inconvenience in my opinion.

Now, Pucallpa has partly paved streets (with a degree of canalization), electricity, and a good airport. The infrastructure is improving, and the city now numbers approximately five hundred thousand inhabitants. It is the second largest jungle city in Peru, the largest being Iquitos in the north. The incoming people have totally changed the character of the city to its advantage and disadvantage. The Amazon hospital is now a government hospital, but it still serves the population of Yarina and part of Pucallpa.

For me, this area of the Peruvian jungle, especially along the many small rivers, remains a corner of the world to which I can retreat, even though modern commerce, terrorists, and guerilleros are increasingly disturbing the peacefulness of times gone by. I left this beautiful spot of the world to continue my residency training in obstetrics and gynecology, but I intended to come back with more medical knowledge. Indeed I did come back, at least five times over the ensuing years, and it was always stimulating. In the late 1960s, we began to deliver babies, mainly as outpatients, in the squatting position. Today the hospital has a very active gyne-obstetrical department and does around three thousand deliveries per year.

MY CHRISTMAS CARD IN 2008

▶ For many years I belonged to the wonderful San Diego Tennis and Racquet Club, where I played a lot of tennis, swam, and worked out on a daily basis; I also enjoyed wonderful social events with other members. It was almost like a very friendly fraternity with beautiful facilities, and my children Todd and Dana enjoyed it as well.

In early December 2008 I went to the club and sat by the fire and started writing Christmas cards. I had a personal address book from A to Z and carefully went through each page. When I came to Lisa's name, I thought of her as I did every Christmas, or whenever I randomly came across her name, but I immediately turned the page and started writing the next card. To this day I do not know why, but for some reason, for the first time in forty-three years, I turned back to her name and found myself staring at the page. The longer I looked at her name, the more memories of my darling Lisa came flooding back to me. I could still see and feel the beautiful, athletic girl that I loved so dearly. The closeness and laughter and wonderful adventures we had truly seemed like yesterday; a feeling of beautiful and unrequited love welled up inside me and I knew I had to write her. I had no idea if she would receive the card, since I didn't know in what part of the world she might be. The only address I had these many years was the same Frauenklinik in Kiel. I wrote a brief personal message and enclosed my business card with my e-mail address, in the unlikely event that she would receive it. On the envelope, I wrote "Please forward" and mailed it. That night I could not get her out of my mind. I wondered what she would think if in fact she did receive it. I knew deeply that I still loved her.

Approximately, five weeks went by and in the middle part of January 2009, I unexpectedly received an e-mail from none other than Lisa. My heart was pounding as I read it. Little did I know she had earlier told her secretary, Sylvia, to throw away all the Christmas cards; she received so many at her clinical address, mostly from medical colleagues and businesses. But Sylvia told her there were a few personal cards she should read. The hand of fate is a mysterious and sometimes wonderful element of life.

Date: Monday, January 26, 2009, 1:51 p.m.
From: Liselotte Mettler
To: <u>Elwin Law</u>
Subject: long, long ago

Dear John,
What a surprise to suddenly hear from you again. I sit at the fireplace and it is snowing here in Kiel, the ocean is covered with some ice formations and life is but a dream. As I have been traveling for some days, my secretary keeps the mail in files and just this afternoon I found your card. I think many floods have gone under the bridge of life, but I still remember you. Greetings, Lilo

She described how her husband had died some four years earlier, that she had three children, and that so much water had crossed under the bridge in these many years. Perhaps the most touching thing she wrote was that she still had our red and black blanket after all these years. I wrote her back immediately, telling her about various personal events in my life. She wrote again saying that she would be in Miami and then Orlando, Florida for a medical conference. I wondered how we might meet. A week later when she was with her children in Miami, I received a call from her. Her voice and wonderful enthusiasm sounded just as it did forty years earlier. She touched a very responsive chord within me. She later told me that my voice evoked a responsive chord in her as well. I asked when she was coming to California, and she said she wasn't but that she would be in Orlando. Something prompted me to ask if I should come down, and she quickly replied, "Yes."

My children thought I was crazy to go to Orlando for one and a half days to see someone I had not seen in forty years. I totally agreed, but said that I really felt drawn to do this. When a window is opened in life, it usually does not remain open for very long.

It was an exciting plane trip from San Diego to Orlando. Later that night, I approached her hotel door with a high level of anticipation. I was not really looking for a relationship and neither was she. I thought we could at least have a nice reunion and reflect on all that had happened in our lives.

I wondered, as I walked to the door, how she looked, and if I would recognize her. I gave the door three short knocks and, as she opened it, my heart pounded. There she stood, hardly having changed at all. Certainly we were both older, but we had both kept ourselves in good physical condition. Her face was beaming with her own broad smile, which I had well remembered. We embraced briefly and exchanged very warm greetings. I could not believe how good and fit she looked—I had forgotten that in her youth she had been a world-class Olympic swimmer for Germany at the Rome Olympics.

We sat on the little couch opposite two large beds. The window to our left gave us a lovely view of the lake below. We talked with great excitement, which was interrupted by occasional hugs. It was obvious to both of us that we still shared a connection and an attraction. We put that aside and kept exchanging stories of all that had happened to us over the years.

Finally, we could resist no longer. I looked at her and she looked deeply at me, and we walked toward the bed. The sexual closeness, arousal, and fulfillment were very beautiful and somehow closer and better than either of us remembered. Neither of us wanted this to end. I told her what I truly felt—that I had never stopped loving her, that my love was somehow put to sleep those many years.

It was a sad good-bye a day and a half later, and we spoke of meeting again as soon as possible, but we were not sure when.

On the flight back to San Diego, I felt that Lisa was very close beside me. I thought of her first e-mail to me entitled "Long, Long Ago." To me it was a beautiful and meaningful title, and I wrote her a poem on the plane entitled "Long, Long Ago."

We wrote each other by e-mail frequently. We were both feeling our way through the lovely woods of our past, and now, our present.

LOVE AND LIFE AT SEVENTY

My first trip to Kiel to see Lisa was one of wonderful anticipation. It had been many years since I had been to Germany, and I was looking forward to the change from California, to say nothing about the excitement of the unknown and known with my love.

The American Airlines flight from San Diego to Hamburg via Dallas went quickly and smoothly. Kiel used to have its own airport, but they closed for lack of traffic. Hamburg is approximately sixty miles south. When I landed, Lisa was there to meet me with her beautiful smile and energetic wave. We embraced briefly and hurried to her car. It was a lovely late autumn day; the weather was just turning a bit cooler. The drive on the autobahn was somewhat scary with cars whizzing by at top speed. If we were even a little slow in moving out of the fast lane, the drivers would blink their lights insistently and drive up within a few feet of our rear—not much had changed over the years.

Automobiles for Germans are not only their prized possessions, which they constantly pamper and polish, but they are also driven like weapons and serve as symbols of authority. The old saying, "The Hun is either at your throat or at your feet," still seemed to hold true, although I did notice a hint of softening in the German demeanor and attitude. They are quite wonderful people and can be friends for life once they accept you. They have their quirks and characteristics as we all do. It was interesting how Lisa really did not share these same characteristics. She was a strong and forceful woman, but also incredibly caring and warm. She truly was a citizen of the world and loved by all.

LISA'S HOME IN KIEL

Many thoughts and memories came flooding back to me as we as we sped down the freeway. I remembered the beautiful green and lush countryside with cows grazing in the distance. Sitting beside her became a comfortable blur of excitement, closeness, and appreciation for this blessing in life.

We arrived at the lovely city of Kiel, which is directly on the Baltic Sea and has a population of about 250,000.

The city was totally destroyed during World War II by the allies, since it was the submarine-manufacturing center of the German navy. Even the Frauenklinik, where she practiced, was severely damaged. Kiel is also famous for its Kiel Canal, which connects the Baltic Sea to the North Sea.

It was a beautiful drive through an old and wooded part of Kiel up to Lisa's long driveway. She had a beautiful, large home directly overlooking the Baltic, which was approximately two hundred yards away. It had a spectacular view, and it was clear Lisa loved her home. She would often entertain numerous medical colleagues from all over the world who would come to Kiel for short periods of study. She was a professor, as well as a teacher and lecturer at the nearby Frauenklinik.

As we got out of the car, she said, "John, come with me to the garden for a moment. I want us to sit together on a special handmade bench and look out over the water." It was truly magnificent. We sat there quietly for about ten minutes. Finally she said, "I want you to feel completely at home here, and let me know of anything you need." I smiled at her and said that all I really needed was to hold her and love her.

She is so beautifully responsive and she took my hand as we went into the house. Our closeness in bed was wonderful. "I can't believe the first thing you do is take me to bed," I whispered.

"It was your idea," she chided, as she stretched toward the ceiling.

"I think I will sleep for a bit, darling. Is that okay?"

"Of course, mein Schatz," she said softly. "I will be downstairs."

I quickly felt totally comfortable in Germany and in Lisa's home. She prepared beautiful meals that we enjoyed by the fire in the evenings, which were rather cool. In the mornings, the view of the magnificent cruise ships and ocean liners going by just in front of the house was quite spectacular. We talked of one day taking a cruise to Norway. I felt sure it would happen.

It was all lovely and intoxicating, and yet our feet seemed firmly on the ground. All of her friends and medical colleagues were most accepting and gracious toward me. I came to find out that Lisa had become a world-renowned gynecologist and was highly respected in many countries. She had written six books and seven hundred medical articles.

It was a sad and emotional moment two weeks later when we said our good-bye. We knew we would meet again, but we didn't know when or where. It was as if our love had taken on a new life of its own and nothing could break it, not even our own occasional blow-ups, which never lasted long. She told me on more than one occasion that I was also her best friend.

As the months passed, they were mixed with travel as well as Lisa's short visits to La Jolla. She and Todd, Dana, Sarah, and Aramis got along beautifully. My children, Todd and Dana, who were thirty-two and twenty-nine respectively, loved her and found her great fun and totally down-to-earth. We all enjoyed lovely BBQs together overlooking the La Jolla Cove, with wonderful conversations and laughter. Life was good. I kept thinking of the saying, "Life is like sailing—it's never in a straight line." In Spain, we enjoyed the wedding of Dana's best friend in Leon and drove through this beautiful country.

I was usually away from La Jolla four to five weeks at a time. I still had my own real estate business to take care of. When we were apart, we wrote each other e-mails nearly every day.

Datum: Wed., 28 Oct 2009 12:03:18
Von: Elwin Law
An: Liselotte Mettler
Betreff: Re: the Law-Mettler family

My Darling Lilo,

I know you are on your way to Florence—Dana's favourite city must be beautiful. I've never been there—would love to go. The time is getting shorter every day until I am with my love. This is a short note to tell you how much I love and adore you and I am so close to you. So much to do—will write longer later.

Dein Johann

Datum: Fri, 30 Oct 2009 09:01:36
Von: Elwin Law
An: Liselotte Mettler
Betreff: Re: the Law-Mettler family

Good morning, my precious,

So glad you are safely in Florence. I am sure it is beautiful. Are you speaking there? I gave Dana the message, which she very much appreciated. All is coming together here—doctor, therapist, moving, working, exercise. I just came from the club—the weather is quite cool. Please come close to me so I can hold you and give you a kiss—two more weeks!!! Darling, ironically your friend Neil and his German wife (who speaks no German) will be in Dubai the same time we are there and would love to see us if it can work out—nice people. Will it be warm anywhere we are going? Still waiting for visa. You are so dear and close to me. Know that I am totally with you and love you with all my heart.

J.

Date: Saturday, October 31, 2009, 1:25 PM
From: Liselotte Mettler
Subject: Re: the Law-Mettler family
To: Elwin Law

Good evening John,

It is 9:00 p.m. here in Kiel, and I am so glad to be back in my surroundings, although it is only for a few days. So, in two weeks we'll hopefully meet in Orlando. I am so much looking forward to it and try to come very close to you right now. It looks like Halloween night in Germany is tonight. How was it at the club? It will be so nice to meet with your friends in Dubai. We'll be there together Dec. 4–10, 2009. The meeting with Brigitte and Peter was very nice today; they send you greetings. They will be in Berlin until Nov. 18, but we will only get there Nov. 20.

Darling, it was great to talk to you last night. I love you so much and really tender and send you myself, as much as one can by e-mail, alles Liebe und bis bald,

Deine Lilo

Date: Saturday, October 31, 2009
From: Elwin Law
To: Liselotte Mettler

My Lilo,

It was wonderful to hear your voice and to "feel" you by phone yesterday. It was intimate and close and loving. I know you are glad to be back in Kiel and your surroundings for a few days. I love you, my darling—two more weeks and we will be together. The move has gone well. Now I have to create places to put things—perhaps another round of disposing. What time do you arrive in Orlando? Let me know the details

when you have them. Isn't all of this wonderful? What beauty and joy. My kiss and dearest love.
Dein Johan

Date: 1 November 2009 18:46:18 CET
From: Elwin Law
Subject: Re: the Law-Mettler family
To: Liselotte Mettler
It touches me deeply to know that you can share special feelings with me about Reza and reflections and all things that are part of life. I feel that I can also share everything of my life with you, my darling.

It is a beautiful, warm sunny day here. Just came from the club. We are all getting together to watch football today and later I have been invited to the home of a friend of mine in the country, Roger Brown, to have a salmon dinner.

Many years ago I loaned him a beautiful dark blue German overcoat when he went to Germany. We have been good friends for many years. He is somewhat of an intellectual and we have fun and similar points of view when we talk. Sweetheart, you would not believe it—yesterday I came across a couple of letters from you and a postcard of a place we stayed in the snow. I think in Austria, every place I look it seems you are there. We will have a literary and pictorial feast when we return to San Diego. I will see you in 13 days, my love. Know that I am with you very closely and always will be.
Johann

Datum: Mon, 19 April 2010 10:10:04–0700 (PDT)

Von: Elwin Law
An: Liselotte Mettler
Betreff: Re: April is a month of work and truth

My dearest love to you, my precious girl. Let me know what your travel plans are back to Kiel as they develop. Both my sisters called yesterday and my Richmond Sister said she also is very strong-willed and will not take no for an answer concerning our visit this year. I told her it is very much our intention to come. I love you and kiss you with all my heart.
Johann

Date: Tuesday, April 20, 2010, 07:05 p.m.
From: Liselotte Mettler
Subject: Re: April is a month of work and truth
To: Elwin Law

My love, I travel in 3 hours back to Kiel and hope to get there safely Emirates. This is their first flight to Hamburg again. You are always with me.
Deine Lilo
I hope that you are well!!! Because only you are my special love and best friend in this world…

Datum: Wed, 21 April 2010 14:13:35–0700 (PDT)
Von: Elwin Law
An: Liselotte Mettler
Betreff: Re: April is a month of work and truth

My precious,
So glad to hear from you. I hope and pray you are safe. I will call you. Spent much of day at Neil's condo. I am now dashing to physiotherapy; will write longer later. All my dearest love.

Dein Johan

Date: Thursday, April 22, 2010, 06:43 a.m.
From: Liselotte Mettler
Subject: Re: April is a month of work and truth
To: Elwin Law
Dear John,
After I heard your voice, I was quiet and peaceful with everyone yesterday. Darling, thank you for calling, and take the best care of yourself. I am happy and full in action back here in Kiel. My time with you was great and wonderful. It gets better every time and I love it.
Bussi,
Lilo
Now I run for a medical faculty meeting where I give a short statement this afternoon—it is 4:00 p.m.

Datum: Friday, 23 April 2010, 10:06:26–0700 (PDT)
Von: Elwin Law
An: Liselotte Mettler
Betreff: Re: April is a month of work and truth
Hello, my darling Citizen of the World. Are you glad to be back in Deutschland? I think of you constantly and miss you so very much. I will see you in 4 weeks down under. I love you with all my heart.
Juanito

Date: Friday, April 23, 2010, 03:17 p.m.
From: Liselotte Mettler
Subject: Re: April is a month of work and truth

To: Elwin Law

Dearest,

I had a wonderful time in Kiel, flew this morning to Düsseldorf, and drove then to some kind of a resort outside of Leverkusen—lovely landscape. Gave a lecture, had a good dinner, and also some clarinet music—a good and interesting performer, good camaraderie, and found my way to the Internet just now. I loved to read your letters and return my good feelings to you, darling, but do not feel committed to meet me in Australia, if down under is time-wise not good for you. We can meet later any time you feel free to do so; you know my schedule more or less, and I am always happy if you can join me. Please try to at least keep the Oman date for the beginning of June, anyway—as we said—in 2 weeks we'll come back to this discussion. Tomorrow morning I'll fly from Düsseldorf to Pristina in Kosovo, and on Sunday afternoon back to Hamburg via Budapest.

I met a very interesting medical couple from Rochester, Minnesota, this evening at our meeting and plan to keep in good contact with them. Did you know that evidently only 15 percent of Americans have passports and travel abroad? The rest seem to live with only their driver's licenses? Talked with Peter a lot over the phone and will try to meet him before he leaves for San Diego. I have the impression that he is not very healthy. They plan a diet health trip together in Austria this summer—thank God we do not have this problem. I am at a good 60 kg and hope to stay there with your help. I still enjoy some side trips, as you know quite well! Now I see you laughing, John. I love you dearly and kiss you long, long, long.

Deine Lilo

Datum: Sun, 25 April 2010 10:07:59–0700 (PDT)
Von: Elwin Law
An: Liselotte Mettler
Betreff: Re: April is a month of work and truth
Fly well wherever you are, my love—Happy Sunday morning—at least here—This is just a short kiss. Hello—
All my love,
Juanito

Date: Sunday, April 25, 2010, 04:30 p.m.
From: Liselotte Mettler
To: Elwin Law
Subject: April is a month of work and truth
Hello my dear John,
Just back from Kosovo—a real interesting country with difficult recent history; they have only been for 3 years and the Serbs have killed so many of them—well, there are many things I saw besides medical issues…we can just be happy to live in a more or less organized world. There was no Internet available. At home I had a good talk with Firus; we looked at the Copper Mountain pictures and did have a good chat until now, two o'clock in the morning. Firus is off to Frankfurt again in the late morning, and we had not seen each other in a long time. Darling, I love you and will only come back with the traveling deals to you after 10 days, as you should not worry about these things and just concentrate on your activities. You do not need to come to Australia if you are in the middle of a deal and can join me at any time later in June or July if that suits you better. This morning at 7:45 I'll have to be at our morning discussion in the clinic, as we are discussing our

next endoscopy courses and that's fine; things are moving and I like that. You are with me always, and I really want to marry you with all my love,

Deine Lilo

Date: Tuesday, April 27, 2010 01:44 a.m.
From: Elwin Law
To: Liselotte Mettler
Subject: Re: April is a month of work and truth

I am so glad you are back safely—I miss you very much, my love. I am trying to do everything possible here. Several showings of Neil's condo but no offers yet. I think it is a little overpriced, but he needs to try this. All possible coverage is being given to it for selling. I feel so much the time is right to get married. That is something I deeply feel in my heart! You are so close to me and such a part of me. I can practically feel you this minute. Take care, my precious girl, and know that I am always there beside you.

My dearest love,

Johann

Date: Saturday, October 09, 2010, 12:37 p.m.
From: Lilo Mettler
To: Elwin Law
Subject: Re: about 2 months before our marriage

Darling, I am also totally with you and will love to marry you; had great experiences today again sailing with Firus and the boys, always excitement, calamities, rescue and so on—we ran out of petrol—the indicators were out of order, that's why the motor striked—another experience with near calamities today; Firus nearly totally lost his balance and became my little boy again. He is completely with us now, has his own problems, which he needs to solve, something I cannot help him with.

Has the lower part of your sister's house in Bequia been restored? Can people live in it? How is Elanne?? Do you hear from Lee and her husband? Have a good weekend and miss me a lot because I miss you, my love. In my thoughts, I am always with you,

Deine Lilo

Date: 12 October 2010, 20:00:11 CEST
From: Elwin Law
To: Lilo Mettler
Subject: Re: about 2 months before our marriage

WOMAN!!! You NEED me there with you to keep you out of all this danger and these near calamities. What am I going to do with you??? We need to be together soon, my adventurous one. Berta and Robert plan to stay in the lower house, which will be fun. They will get there before we do. I am in close touch with Lee. They have made their move to the other house. All is well there. My sister has deteriorated greatly—can hardly speak on the phone—So glad we had this visit together. You were wonderful! Why don't you stay away from the boat for a while? Is the universe trying to tell you something?? I worry about my Love. Nothing—nothing—may happen to you. Remember, it is not only your well-being, but now it is very much mine and vice versa. This is a letter of love chastisement. You know how precious you are to me. When do you go to Dubai? I love my precious with all my life—God keep you safe.

Your Love

The special closeness we felt, even several thousand miles apart, was incredibly strong. I loved her very deeply, and I trusted totally our love and commitment to each other. I knew she felt the same. Our souls and hearts touched deeply.

LISA'S PROFESSIONAL WORLD

Our travels together took us far and wide with Lisa's medical conferences and responsibilities. I would tell people that I was her bodyguard, which they seemed to enjoy. Our times in Kiel were always interesting and my German seemed to be improving. I knew it was still far from what it should be or what I wanted it to be, but people appeared to understand me quite well. One of my favorite places in Kiel was the Alt Stadt (Old Town), which was lovely and quaint with its St. Nikolai Church. One of my favorite authentic places was the historical Kieler Brauerei, which was a dimly lighted restaurant with excellent food. They also made their own wonderful beer in the basement below. In front of St. Nikolai's is the famous Barlach Angel. No one knows if the angel is descending from heaven or ascending from hell. I also enjoyed Kieler Woche (Kiel Week), which is celebrated annually. It is a week of fantastic festivities and parties and the largest sailing races in the world, with over fifty countries represented and competing; it's truly a unique experience.

We mixed business with great pleasure on our trips, traveling to fascinating places such as Dubai, which bubbled with luxury and international flavor. One could see a very conservative, traditional woman wearing an abaya and veil walking alongside a beautiful Arab woman in a miniskirt. Prayers were strictly observed five times a day. So many of the hotels were dripping with opulence and excellent food. The people were very polite and friendly. One of the very interesting areas was the Gold Such (Gold Area), where there was nothing but block after block of jewelry stores jammed together, displaying an abundance of gold, silver, diamonds, and jewelry of every sort for sale. I felt like a kid in a candy store the size of Wal-Mart.

Lisa also performed surgery in Bahrain, which at that time was very safe, peaceful, and stable. Little did we suspect the turmoil and unrest bubbling just beneath the surface. The United States' fifth fleet is also stationed there, and the sailors I spoke with seemed very happy with their surroundings. Lisa's medical colleagues there were most gracious and welcoming. Saudi Arabia was just a few miles away, separated from Dubai by a fifteen-mile bridge.

We also went to Oman, which was most interesting, as well as Kiev in the Ukraine with its magnificent and beautiful architecture of gold-domed churches and buildings. We were in Kiev in the cold, snowy winter. I would love to experience this wonderful city in the summer.

After a conference in Sydney, we went to one of the most interesting and romantic places in the north of Australia. This was Green Island on the Great Barrier Reef. It is a very small island close to Cairns, about a forty-five minute boat ride away. The beauty, peace, and quiet would melt any heart. Swimming on the Great Barrier Reef was an exhilarating experience; Lisa was in heaven.

We also traveled to Indonesia, Bali, Hong Kong, and India. A very special experience was our trip to Pune, India, where one of Lisa's favorite former students, Shailesh, is a top surgeon. The third day we were there, he said to Lisa, "I want to take you tomorrow morning to a special place." Four of us drove in his car to a beautiful remote area forty-five minutes outside of Pune, where there was already a partially built world-class combination of a university and medical facilities. Shailesh said to Lisa, as we stood a thousand feet high overlooking a beautiful green valley and golf course in the distance, "Over here, on this spot, we will build a world-class hospital, and I wish to name the hospital for you and in your honor." We were both extremely moved. She smiled at him with sincere gratitude.

A unique and most interesting experience was a personal side tip we took to Putaparthi, where we attended a ten-thousand-person gathering with the holy man and avatar, Sai Baba (also called Swami). Many people there worship him like a god. I think of the old saying, "There are many paths to the top of the mountain, but once you are there, the view is the same." Lisa and I both enjoyed this entirely new experience and the unbelievable peace and quiet of the town and the people, but after three days we knew we were quite happy and fulfilled with our own beliefs.

One can truly get to know another during extensive traveling. It can be extremely romantic, exciting, and adventurous, but it can also be very grueling, demanding, and exhausting with airports, security, and all-night trips. It either brings one closer together or totally apart. We were very fortunate to have grown closer in the trenches.

DECISIONS

After two years, we both knew we wanted to marry and spend our lives together. Lisa and I, for sure, had our moments of ups and downs. We are both very strong people with our own ways and characteristics, but our relationship evolved and we grew more and more harmonious. We never forgot—even in heated moments—that we truly loved each other.

On our trip to Sydney, we decided to walk through the streets and do some window-shopping for rings. She had never before worn an engagement or wedding ring. We passed by this beautiful jewelry store with lovely diamonds in the window. I asked her, "Is there any special ring that appeals to you?"

She immediately responded, "I don't want one of those shiny things that stick up on top. I want only a simple gold band, something comfortable, and if I am going to get a ring, I would like for you to have the same and wear it as an engagement ring as I will." I tried to explain to her that boys didn't wear engagement rings, only girls. She said she didn't care, and that we should break tradition and both wear them before the wedding. She was too charming and loving to refuse.

It was a late afternoon in Kiel; the weather was somewhat warm. I wore white pants and a blue blazer. Lisa had on a lovely blue dress, and we were quite careful as we climbed aboard her sailboat, which was docked at the harbor. We were totally alone, and we looked lovingly at each other as we sat across the table down below. Yes, I got down on one knee and asked her with all my heart to marry me. She smiled and said yes. We toasted with a glass of champagne and we embraced, both feeling a special closeness. Later, we joined her son, Moritz, and six other very close friends at the nearby yacht club and had a lovely dinner.

My dear sister, Elanne, with whom I was very close all my life, gave her home for our wedding reception on the island of Bequia in the Grenadines, approximately one hundred miles from Barbados.

Lisa and I had visited there once, and she fell in love with the place. We were married there in a lovely, simple little church on top of a mountain with a lovely view of the Caribbean. Our family, along with approximately forty close friends from many places, celebrated this special occasion with us on December 4, 2010. It was a special honor and pleasure to have had an occasion with Sir James Mitchell, who had been Prime Minister for many years and who had made wonderful contributions to the island. He had also been a friend of my sister.

RECONNECTION WITH JOHN IN 2009 FROM LISA'S POINT OF VIEW

▶▶ When we celebrated the coming of the new century in the year 2000, I tried to remember my life during the twentieth century and had one short flash of my American boyfriend from the late 1960s, John.

What had happened to him? Did he marry his German girlfriend Margarete who, during our year of love, was waiting for him in California? Did he marry an actress or one of the secretaries who adored him in his American office in Munich? Did he have children? Did he ever remember me? He was from Georgia but also liked California. Where was he living now? I had put his blanket on our sailboat, Okeanos, a forty-three-foot Nauticat, with which we traveled the Baltic Sea on many occasions, from Kiel to Denmark and Sweden. I still liked to cover myself at nights with his blanket. My life was fulfilling and good.

After Reza's sudden death, I was devastated, and in spite of the love of my children, I was very lonely in the following years. I had a close relationship with my three boys, Bijan, Firus, and Moritz. They all developed nicely in their professional careers and characters. We met frequently and enjoyed each other's company. I love being a grandmother to Bijan's three children, but, of course, I cannot always be with them.

After reaching retirement age in Germany, I entered upon a new, very active professional life. In 2006 I started to work in Dubai as a visiting professor in the German Medical Center at the Dubai Healthcare City (DHCC). My activities in Dubai focus on endoscopic surgery, and I continue to work there regularly for one week every month. In Kiel, I still have an office at the University's Department of Obstetrics and Gynecology and am engaged in teaching and research. I receive many invitations to lecture and operate around the world and have been awarded honorary memberships to many professional medical societies.

I have wonderful professional friends and a lovely family. In the summer of 2008, my youngest son, Moritz, then twenty years old, left Kiel to begin his studies in Miami, Florida. At home, I was alone, although I traveled a lot. I rejected many well-meant invitations from male friends. I seemed not to want them or need them; life was still busy.

After a pleasant Christmas and New Year in Kiel and a skiing trip in the Austrian Alps with the children and their friends and families, I went for a week to Dubai and to Bahrain for endoscopic surgery and lectures. I then had a meeting in Bruneck with my friend, Dr. Bruno Engl, on the topic of endometriosis. We were forty gynecologists and managed to fit in a little skiing in the beautiful Dolomites.

Back in Kiel, my office manager, Sylvia said, "At last you are back. Besides your involvement in the current endoscopic teaching course and all of the manuscripts and e-mails we have to work on, there are a lot of Christmas cards from pharmaceutical and industrial companies you should look at."

I said, "Sylvia, this year there's no time. Just throw them away."

"But, Lisa," she answered, "there are some cards with personal handwritten notes."

"Okay," I said. "Pack them into a folder and I'll look at them tonight at home."

It was a cold, late January evening. I lit the fire and prepared black tea with rum to warm myself. First, I corrected an essay of one of my PhD students, and then I opened the file with the Christmas cards. There, I found the card from John, my boyfriend of long ago, with his business card: Elwin Law, real estate, La Jolla, California. He had also included his picture with his CV and his e-mail address. Interesting, I thought. I have often been to La Jolla for conferences and my son Firus spent a year in the Army and Navy Academy, a military boarding school, in nearby Carlsbad. But I had never contacted John.

That same evening I wrote John an e-mail, thanking him for contacting me. "Much water has passed under the bridge since we last met," I wrote. "How are you doing?"

I mentioned that I was unfortunately a widow, had three boys, and still enjoyed life, and I sent all the best and kindest regards. This was the beginning of a long e-mail correspondence.

He answered quickly, asking in the e-mail if I ever come to the USA. I said I would be in Miami next week to see my children, Bijan and Moritz, and also to attend a conference in Orlando, Florida. He told me to call him when I arrived there, and he gave me his phone number. In his picture, he still looked quite sharp.

A week later, in early February 2009, I called him from Miami. Hearing his strong voice made me feel excited and happy. It was a firm and familiar tone from the past. My heart seemed to open; I smiled and laughed while I was talking to him. He asked, "Are you coming to California?" I answered that this was absolutely not on my itinerary. "Why are you laughing?" he asked. I had no answer. His reply was, "Let me see if I can come to see you."

"Do you want to visit me during my four days in Miami or during the three days in Orlando?" I asked. I had to fly out directly after the conference in Orlando via New York to Dubai. The reply was, "I will come to Orlando to see you without your children. Can I stay with you?" he continued.

Without any reflection, I said yes and described where we could meet at the Disney resort.

My answer came spontaneously, and I don't know why I was so direct. I normally wouldn't be on an occasion like that. I was very excited to meet him, but I did not mention any of this to the children. The next time I spoke to John on the phone, he told me, "Just start with your conference and I will come on the second day." I gave him my room number and explained about taking the Magic Express from the Orlando airport to the resort.

After I had arrived on the Magic Express, I booked a seat for John and told the lady at the reservation counter that tomorrow my friend, Elwin Law, would arrive from California. The lady said, "Okay, honey," and took down his name. When John arrived, he checked in with the same lady and asked her, "How does my fiancée look?" The lady found this strange, but replied, "Very well and nice." John then explained to her that he hadn't seen me for forty-two years and was interested to know how I looked. Some hours later he rang the bell of my hotel room.

We had had a conference reception that evening, and John had told me he would arrive after 10:00 p.m. I told my colleagues that I would be seeing a boyfriend from the past that evening. They appeared to be worried.

"Why are you not meeting him in the lobby?" they asked. "You've no idea what he might be up to."

"Well it's too late now," I said. "I can't reach him anymore." Annie, the wife of my dear friend Maurice, gave me her room number to ring if I needed help.

My heart was pounding as I opened the door. Outside, there was music on the lake and a funny boat parade. There John stood, as tall as I remembered, with that wonderful, jolly smile. "Hello," he said, "here I am." We looked at each other and embraced briefly.

"Come in, there's a boat parade outside. Let's look at it," I said and guided him to the little balcony. Then we sat down on the couch and I offered him a drink. "Water is fine," he said. Okay, I thought, maybe he doesn't drink alcohol. I poured myself a Coke. We told each other how we lived, what we were doing now, and we talked about life in general.

Suddenly, he asked, "Do you have a laptop, and is there an Internet connection?"

"Yes," I replied, and he clicked onto a website.

"Let's look at this video," he said. There I saw him giving a lecture on how to lose weight while drinking beer.

"Do you drink beer?" I asked.

"Of course," was his answer, and we slightly touched each other for the first time. I felt a flutter of emotions within me but pushed them aside. We talked about our children, his divorce, the sudden death of my husband, and the pain I suffered after that. He touched me very understandingly, and a closeness began to develop.

Finally, I poured him a beer and myself a glass of white wine. The hours went by rapidly, and we tried to remember our life together forty-two years ago. We talked about the blanket I had kept after he left Germany; I had already told him about it in our brief e-mail correspondence. We spoke about feelings, about happiness, and suddenly I felt more and more touched by his presence, and I accepted his touching me with some joy. Later, we kissed each other. I felt like a young girl in the arms of my John in Munich again. We laughed and laughed and suddenly we were lying in bed and holding each other tightly. I looked at my watch; it was way beyond midnight. He touched me so lovingly and kindly that I could only respond with a big hug for him. I forgot my old resentment and my heart opened to John; he pulled me close and loved me that night forever and ever.

We had found each other again. We each had our very different pasts, but each of us seemed to be ready for a new love and a new life together. It became very clear to me when I woke up the next morning and found myself lying in his arms that I had found my old love again. We only had a little more than twenty-four hours together.

The next evening there was a lecture and a banquet for the SLS (Society of Laparoscopic Surgeons) board members and speakers. The small group of our very distinguished board welcomed John in a very pleasant way. They understood how reserved I had been after the death of my husband, Reza, and welcomed my new love. There were tremendous fireworks outside, and despite the noise, we talked with lots of people. We went swimming, took a boat, lay down in a hammock, and looked at each other.

After the next night, we just had a short breakfast together and then had to separate. There were tears in our eyes when we said good-bye. I flew to Dubai via New York, and John flew back to San Diego. The love we felt was immense, and we both wanted it to continue. How to make that happen was something we didn't know at that moment, but we were certain we were not going to let another forty years go by, not at the ages of sixty-nine and seventy. This proved to be a wise decision.

On his flight back to San Diego, John wrote me a poem, a wonderful love poem. I wrote him a long e-mail with suggestions for dates and times to see and feel each other again. This was the first e-mail I had ever sent from an airplane. It contained all the divine inspirations you can have in a 380 airbus, an Emirates double-decker plane that flew me from New York's Kennedy Airport to Dubai in the United Arab Emirates. I knew we had a future together ahead of us and that was wonderful.

We e-mailed and e-mailed.

Date: Thursday, February 18, 2009, 2:11 PM
From: Liselotte Mettler
Subject: Fwd: Re: long, long ago and today
To: Elwin Law
Just landed in Dubai and ready for an early morning start at the German Medical Center. I cannot close my eyes before saying good night to you or, better, good morning in California.
Here is the second picture—I technically do not succeed to send 2 pictures. I suppose I have to learn more from my children, but with the MAC computer, everything is different.
Love
LILO

Datum: Thu, 19 Feb 2009 14:30:22–0800 (PST)
Von: Elwin Law
An: Liselotte Mettler
Betreff: Re: Fwd: Re: long, long ago
Baby—Did you happen to get my white turtleneck from our love room 4413 in Orlando?
—Love-Me, J.

Datum: Thu, 19 Feb 2009 22:59:13 +0100
Von: "Liselotte Mettler"
Betreff: Re: long, long ago and today

Lieber John,
I am fighting with myself not to open my e-mail tonight and to stay away from you, but I lost and before I go to sleep, I want to be with you again, at least through writing to you. I had fabulous experiences these days, professionally everything was quite rewarding—look at these 2 pictures and make up your mind—and emotionally I had tonight a great evening—but I still very much prefer to be with you. Tomorrow I travel for 2 days to Austria, where we'll have, in a beautiful Alpine area, a meeting of the "insiders" on the female disease "endometriosis." I hope to ski there at least for 3 hours.

Date: Monday, February 23, 2009, 12:53 PM
From: Liselotte Mettler
Subject: Re: Fwd: Re: long, long ago and today
To: Elwin Law

Dear John,

Of course I have your white turtleneck as well as another T-shirt—all newly washed and ready for you, with me—as I am still traveling. The whole Austrian short trip was great. I am now again 12 hours away from you back in the Gulf area with the time of 23 hours at present time on Monday evening. I am in Bahrain. This is a tropical/desert kingdom—a lot to say about it, but not in this e-mail. Falling oil prices, loss of jobs, also very intensive here, but "luckily" our medical-surgical input seems to be always needed. I have a full program ahead of me and would love to feel your passion. In this context I have a personal and sincere request for you, if health is permitting. You gave me some good advice, like keep your head up, back straight. Now I want to ask you to improve your walking—if from the backside of yours possible—by daily walks/runs on the treadmill, slowly advancing your speed. That is for your health important, and, for both of us, necessary. Tolstoi wrote in one of his novels about the true love of the advanced age, could that have hit us?? Darling, greetings and take good care of yourself. I survived ice-skating and a lovely 2 hours skiing trip in Austria yesterday and send you all my love—with 2 pictures in the attachment.
LILO

Datum: Tue, 24 Feb 2009 11:12:20–0800 (PST)
Von: Elwin Law
An: Liselotte Mettler
Betreff: Re: Fwd: Re: long, long ago and today
My Darling Lilo,

I love you so much! It is interesting how the flower was opened in Orlando and has grown each day so beautifully—I feel we are so close to each other, in spite of the miles apart. I loved your phone call and our talk.

Had a wonderful visit with Peter and Brigitte two days ago at her home. I felt so comfortable with both of them. We spoke so much of you—what did you do in Lyon when you were 18 and Peter would not go to the movies with you????? Also, I will gladly take your advice concerning treadmill—we will keep each other so healthy and in great shape. I loved our closeness and our love—I cannot wait to see you and hold you close

My dearest love,

J.

Datum: Tue, 25 Feb. 2009 1:15.04–07500(PST)
Von: Liselotte Mettler
An: Elwin law
Betreff: long, long ago
Dear John,

Maybe our love has always been there, just not known to either one of us. I felt particularly in the last 3 and a half years, after Reza's death, that there should be someone who still evokes admiration and feelings in me, but I had no answer—I am now nearly sure, totally would be too soon, but I do hope that we really fit each other. Today I briefly talked to one of my quite close friends here in Bahrain, and I will meet him this evening. He has hopes, but I have no feelings for him, just admiration for what he does as a hospital director and truly good surgeon. At 2:30 tomorrow, that is in 7 hours, I will fly back to Germany. I have a 1 day conference in Hamburg and then on Saturday I'll be back in Kiel and I am looking forward to reading your poem.

Isn't life beautiful? I understand that you—maybe—will meet Peter and Brigitte again tomorrow, isn't that a coincidence that we both, my brother and I, have good friends in San Diego now? My greetings to your son and his wife. I have not told anything to my boys as yet, time will come.

Bussi,

LILO

Datum: Wed, 25 Feb 2009 14:36:05–0800 (PST)
Von: Elwin Law
An: Liselotte Mettler
Betreff: Re: Fwd: Re: long, long ago and today

My darling Lilo,

I know we'll be soon together forever, and I am truly looking forward to meeting you in Miami with your boys, Love, love, J.

We met in Miami; La Jolla, California, John's home in the USA; and in Kiel, my home in Germany. We traveled to many wonderful places and countries in the course of my professional medical activities. Everywhere we went, we were received with open arms—in Europe; the United States; in the Arab countries; in the Far East, China and Indonesia; in Australia, and in Hawaii. Best of all, we liked to drive around

Germany and California. Our children and families greatly supported our togetherness and were happy for us.

My youngest son, Moritz, and I became very attached to each other after the sudden demise of Reza. Moritz eventually left Kiel to begin his studies in Miami before I had reconnected with John, but I still cared always too much for him. After he met John he said to me, "Mommy, you let me go my way now, as finally, you are again happy." It was Moritz who led me to the altar at our marriage ceremony on the island of Bequia.

John and I share a common spiritual life and our love of God and life itself. We have a unique appreciation of all religions and beliefs. Our reconnection and love led to the beautiful Caribbean wedding on Bequia in Saint Vincent and the Grenadines. Reverend Devon joined us in marriage on this unique island in the presence of our children, family, and friends in early December 2010. John's sister, Elanne, had lived on the island for a while and, with her blessing, we decided to celebrate our old-new love on her beloved island. She died shortly before our marriage but was the first to receive our marriage invitation in August 2010.

Life is good: demanding and full of love and happiness if you look for it and have the patience and endurance to find it. Together you are stronger than you are alone. This is an old truth, but it is wonderful to be able to feel and live it.

REFLECTIONS ON THE PAST

It was most interesting for me to reflect back on years past. I remembered that my mother had kept John's letters and pictures after he went back to America in her house in Stuttgart. After I married in 1970, she never spoke of John again, but when she moved out of the apartment in 1985, she suddenly asked me what she should do with John's letters and pictures. "Just throw them away," I said as John and I had had no contact in forty-two years.

I had raised three sons and three nephews and was happily married until Reza's death in 2005. The only memento of John I had kept was his black and red blanket, one of his most prized belongings, which he had given to me when he left Germany in 1968. It had been an emotional and difficult good-bye in Hamburg. My sons knew it as the blanket of Lisa's past.

On one of John's visits to Kiel in the last two years, he wrote a poem about this lovely blanket that is now covering us again:

The Blanket

I have covered you both for many a year—
With occasional sadness, but mostly great cheer—

It is wonderful you are back
And together again—
When you lie on me,
I smile and I grin.

Let's all stay close
And let me keep you warm—

May you always be safe
And shielded from harm.
My love (the blanket)

John's daughter, Dana, one day long after the divorce of her parents, volunteered to sort out John's pictures of the past and put them into albums for his birthday. She knew nothing of our love. After reconnecting in 2009, John showed me the albums, which he had never really appreciated, on one of my visits to La Jolla. All of a sudden, we found many pictures of the two of us in Munich, Hamburg, Stuttgart, and Kiel, and even a picture of our parting in Hamburg in 1968, when I took the blanket and looked at him with all my love. What a wonderful job Dana did of putting faces that looked similar together. Thanks to her, I could see, forty-two years later, that

I looked at John with loving eyes in 1968. What a sweet daughter I now have in Dana, with her nice husband Aramis; I never had a daughter before.

With Todd, John's son, and his wife Sarah, I inherited two additional lovely children and thank God for them.

HIGHLIGHTS OF 2009 AND 2010, AFTER RECONNECTING WITH JOHN

Our second rendezvous in Miami took place over Easter 2009. I flew to Miami, very excited, and spent the first two days alone with my two children and family who live in Miami. On the phone we had decided that John should come straight to Moritz's apartment. At the time, he was a medical student. Luckily, John arrived before Moritz returned from school.

We had exchanged many loving and passionate e-mails, but I still felt my heart pounding and nearly bursting. All of a sudden, John was there with his bright smile, looking as if he controlled the whole situation perfectly. We fell into each other's arms. I looked long and deeply into his eyes and forgot everything around us. I think we both cried, as everything was so emotional. I felt that I never wanted to lose him again.

We enjoyed the company of the children. All three boys accepted this "old-new" love of their mother with a certain natural reservation, as they still saw me with my late husband Reza, whom we had all loved very much.

John and I enjoyed Miami—we walked the streets, the beaches, went boating with friends, and the days passed like hours. We made plans to be together more often in spite of John's busy life in California and mine in Kiel and Dubai (I still worked in both places). I also had many invitations to hold lectures at medical conferences in Europe, Asia, Africa, Australia, Latin and Central America, Canada, and the United States. My lectures improved and my friends said, "Lisa, you have become much more precise, loving, and friendly." John's love gave me a wonderful harmony in my professional and personal lives. I became even more sympathetic toward my patients, gave them more time to express themselves, became less impatient, and developed into a better teacher, according to my friends and colleagues.

One of my former students invited me to Surabaya, Indonesia, where he had become a director of his unit. While there, I had the pleasure of performing a few laparoscopic surgical procedures, and I also delivered a few lectures. At an evening party, our colleagues asked John and me to sing a song from our country. What could we select? As we both loved spirituals, we decided to sing "Do Lord, oh, do Lord, oh do remember me." Suddenly, the Muslim Indonesians joined us in singing this surprisingly well-known Christian song.

John and I enjoyed Green Island, a lovely island out of Cairns, Australia on the Barrier Reef. We always combined the lectures that I gave with a little privacy. This brought us closer and closer together. In India, we attended medical meetings with thousands of gynecologists and took great pleasure in their hospitality. One of my Indian students is building a university hospital and will name it Lilo Mettler Hospital. I enjoyed seeing the admiration in John's eyes when my former student revealed this to us.

While I was working with patients in Dubai, John was busy on the computer or exploring his surroundings. He never got bored. During some medical lectures when we discussed surgical procedures with pictures and videos, I saw John covering his eyes, as he wished to have no part in these details and did not like to see graphic medical conditions. We missed each other during the months we spent apart, pursuing our own lives and work. Never in my life have I written so many letters, now all by e-mail, and I loved to read his daily responses.

On another visit to India, we tried to follow my sister-in-law's advice and visit Putarparthi, south of Bangalore, for a spiritual confrontation. Prior to this little excursion, I had given an inaugural speech to eight thousand participants at the Annual Indian Conference of the Gynecological Society. The visit to Putarparthi to see Sai Baba, an avantar and god for the ten thousand devotees who visited him daily, brought John and me closer together in our love. It was difficult for us to understand the power of Sai Baba, but this exciting adventure with ten thousand and more believers strengthened our faith in God.

Concerning John's home, I love the life in La Jolla, California, this beautiful small town in San Diego. It has a Euro-American spirit, sunshine, and very friendly people. We had time together to enjoy the ocean and the desert, the mountains, Old Town, and boating. John had his work in real estate but also spent a lot of time showing me around. I felt closest to him there. Daily, we went to his racquet and tennis club, worked out, played tennis and golf, swam, and used the Jacuzzi. What a life! I wrote my best medical papers in our condo and cooked some lovely meals. I loved to entertain John's children and their spouses. I always told him we have to see how we two bachelors, who have lived so many years alone, can harmonize. He just said, "Darling, where there is love, there is life. Forget your thoughts, just live it." I frowned on some of his habits, but they were so "charming" that I could never stay angry for longer than five minutes.

In Kiel, my German hometown, I was mostly very busy in the hospital but also had a lot of invitations from friends and family. In the winter we enjoyed cozy evenings around the open fire. John helped me in so many ways to enjoy my life in Kiel again. He went with me to the cemetery and was indeed very understanding of all the tears I still shed for Reza. One of my boys saw John more in Kiel, the others more in Miami.

We participated in Kiel Week and entertained many guests in our house. In the summer we sailed on our boat Okeanos, (a forty-three-foot sailboat) and my California-Georgia boy learned to love the cold, but lovely, Baltic Sea; he even swam in it. We sailed to different Danish islands, around Seeland, to Copenhagen, Bornholm, and Heiligenhafen. Life became better and closer between us. In July 2010, on board Okeanos, John proposed to me and wrote this lovely promise on a simple sheet of white paper:

I love you, my darling.
In so many ways
Totally without pretense
And personal praise

I pray that this day
You accept this ring
To join hands forever
And embrace all that life brings

Of course, I said yes with all my heart. At seventy-one years old, I felt young and indeed very thankful and happy. We had two small glasses of champagne and then spontaneously invited the children, two of mine were at that time in Kiel, and some friends for a dinner in the Kieler Yacht Club.

The world around us is experiencing so many ups and downs, provoked partly by natural catastrophes but also by continuous political movements for liberty, peace, and power. With the presidency of Barak Obama, America has shown a new face to the world, but inside the country there is a lot of discontent with his government and opposition to his decisions. People seem to want immediate solutions and are not ready to wait years for accomplishments like the health bill. Angela Merkel, as German Chancellor, has to stand up in Europe and the world for our country. It is great and amazing how she is fighting for the continuation of the European Union: nothing is easy and accepted by everyone. Where do we stand? We need a solid love to live and act in this world. Together with John, I am finding my way more easily. I can be a better mother to my children and three grandchildren, and maybe even a better human being.

OUR MARRIAGE

After two years, John and I both knew without any doubt in our hearts or minds that we wanted to get married and join our lives together. For sure we had our occasional ups and downs. We are both very strong people with our own ways, but we had lovingly become harmonious. We both never forgot—even in the most heated moments—that we truly loved each other. The future seemed to open new doors for us.

We decided to marry on the colorful and beautiful Caribbean island of Bequia, belonging to Saint Vincent and the Grenadines, with the blessing of Reverend Devon. We had met this tall, good-looking Black minister on a visit to the island at John's sister's house in the summer of 2010. Reverend Devon serves a small church on a steep hill with tropical trees, vibrant red and yellow flowers, multicolored butterflies, and a magnificent view of the sea from all sides.

On December 4, 2010, we received God's blessing for our life as a married couple in the presence of our children and grandchildren, nephews and nieces, and about forty friends. It was a simple but beautiful church ceremony, high up on Mount Olivet, and we truly felt the love of God to be with us forever.

I wore a locally made long, white dress and John a white suit. My Viennese friend, Daniela, had decorated my hair with violet orchids and in my hands I held a bouquet of orchids.

Throughout the ceremony, while we exchanged beautiful golden rings and promised to be united for better or for worse, I felt waves of blessings running through my body. I heard Reverend Devon's pleasant, mighty voice saying, "This is the day that the love of God unites Lisa and John in the bond of marriage, to be together in good times and in bad times. Do you promise to love each other…" A steel band was playing and accompanied our singing of "Amazing grace, how sweet the sound…"

It was a hot, sunny day and just after everyone had reached the Gingerbread Hotel, where the wedding reception and festivities were to continue, the heavens opened. I found this brief but strong rain shower meaningful and magnificent, as it gave us all the chance to cool down a little.

God has taken us under his protection and into his empire of love, life, and strife. Two in one, that is how we feel and act. We feel powerful together and seem to overcome all problems more easily than before. I have found again the wonderful love and friend of my younger years and now seem to love him more than ever. Every time we need to pursue our life's duties, face confrontations of work, politics, or family, or have to be apart from each other, it hurts, but it also strengthens and intensifies the feelings we have for each other. I feel John is with me wherever I am and in whatever action I am engaged in. We respect each other's duties, obligations, and choices, and give each other, besides our passion for each other, also the freedom and space we need. To have become John's wife is wonderful, and I love him with all my heart.

EPILOGUE

We both believe God has been so good to us. "Life is like sailing—it's never in a straight line." We keep on sailing along between La Jolla on the Pacific Ocean, in California, and Kiel on the Baltic Sea, in Germany, embracing the world.

"Long, Long Ago"

Long, long ago
I saw you sitting there

With your beautiful face and smile
And lovely golden hair.

I asked permission to sit down
And wondered what you'd say.
Across your face came a slight frown,
But your smile said please stay.

There was a connection
From the very start,
As strange as that may be.
There was touching
Deep within the heart,
And a "knowing" of rarity.
Fate closed our book
For a period of time,
Later to be reopened

And rewritten line by line.

When I saw you again,
The connection was still there.
I knew in my heart
There was love and there was care.
February 14, 2009
John

Elwin W. Law

Elwin was born in Thomasville, Georgia and grew up in the South. He excelled in sports as well as receiving numerous other honors. His family was a very well-respected southern family with valued traditions.

Elwin went to Washington and Lee University in Lexington, Virginia and Graduate School in International Business at the Thunderbird in Phoenix, Arizona. He has conversational abilities in four languages.

He was commissioned an officer in the U.S. Army upon graduation from Washington and Lee, and served two years in Germany. First as platoon leader of the 54th Infantry Armored Rifle Battalion in Heilbronn, Germany and then as Commander of Troops of the 4th Armored Division N.C.O. Academy in Neu-Ulm, Germany.

Elwin later was a Stockbroker with Paine-Webber stock brokerage company in Santa Monica, California and then Regional Manager of the Ruhr Gebiet in Germany, with headquarters in Munich of a Los Angeles company.

In 1973 he entered the Real Estate profession with Coldwell-Banker in La Jolla, California and in 1976 established his own company, specializing both in Residential and Investment Properties. He was also elected to the position of Chief Financial Officer and later President of the prestigious Real Estate Brokers Association of La Jolla.

Elwin has two wonderful children, Dana and Todd.

Contact Information: Elwin Law (John)
La Jolla, California, 92038 USA
E-mail: longlongagolovestory@yahoo.com

Liselotte Mettler, Prof. MD, PhD.

Kiel, Germany

E-mail: longlongagolovestory@yahoo.com

Liselotte Mettler was born in Vienna, Austria and studied medicine in Tübingen, Vienna and Kiel, Germany. She swam for Germany at the Olympic Games in Rome in 1960.

Liselotte specialized in obstetrics and gynaecology at the Kiel university department of obstetrics and gynaecology in 1973, completed her postdoctoral lecture qualification in 1976 and was appointed professor in 1981. She is now Professor Emeritus of the Kiel University and Honorary Chair of the Kiel School of Gynecological Endoscopy and Reproductive Medicine. Currently, Liselotte works as a professor at the Dubai Healthcare City and at the Harvard Medical School in Dubai, United Arab Emirates.

After working for two years as a medical doctor in the jungles of Peru, Liselotte carried out several research and clinical periods in Israel, the USA and Great Britain. She is Ex-President of the German and European Societies for Gynaecological Endoscopy, Ex-President of the German Society of Reproductive Medicine and was Scientific Programme Chairman of the International Federation of Fertility Societies (IFFS) Meeting in Munich, Germany in 2010. Liselotte was Honorary Chair at the Meeting of the American Society of Minimal Invasive Gynecology in 2010 in Las Vegas and is General Secretary of the International Academy of Human Reproduction (IAHR), whose next world congress will be held in Venice, Italy in March 2013.

Liselotte has written 20 books and has published over 600 articles in medical journals. She is the mother of three sons, Sebastian-Bijan, Alexander-Firus and Moritz Stefan.

Additional copies available through
www.CreateSpace.com/3731900,
Amazon.com, and other retailers.